Praise for Justin's Work

Justin Wise connects the power of social media with the potential for life-changing ministry in a completely fresh, easy-to-understand, and relevant way. His energy and wisdom bleed through the pages. He gets it. He totally gets it and now you can too. *The Social Church* is a must-read for all Christian leaders called to serve in this time and space.

Tami Heim, president and CEO of Christian Leadership Alliance,
coauthor of *@stickyJesus: How to Live Out Your Faith Online*

The rumors are true: Justin Wise knows his stuff. Not only does he ask the right hard questions in *The Social Church* but he boldly challenges the status quo, encouraging churches to embrace digital communications with vision, strategy, and purpose.

Carrie Kintz, Digital Communication Strategist, Focus on the Family

Justin is a knowledgeable and accomplished practitioner of social media strategy and tactics as well as a practiced speaker on the subject. He consistently creates and publishes useful content that goes beyond mere thoughts and opinions to include the tools he uses for success and the tactics and techniques for others to become successful.

Chris Giovagnoni, Social Media Marketing
Program Manager, Compassion International

Justin Wise is the real deal. He is passionate about local churches and assisting them in connecting with a new generation. He brings creative and innovative thinking to each training, but more than that, you'll find in him a genuine heart of service with a purpose.

Haley Veturis, Social Media Manager, Saddleback Church

Justin has handled social media for both our SCORRE and Platform conferences in the last year and we couldn't be more pleased.

He understands the power of social media and the benefits that come when it's used correctly. Most importantly, he accomplished our goal: people who weren't at the event felt like they were and were encouraged to sign up for the next one.

Michael Hyatt, New York Times bestselling author,
former CEO of Thomas Nelson Publishers

the SOCIAL CHURCH

a THEOLOGY of DIGITAL COMMUNICATION

the SOCIAL CHURCH

a THEOLOGY of DIGITAL COMMUNICATION

JUSTIN WISE

MOODY PUBLISHERS

CHICAGO

All Scripture quotations, unless otherwise indicated, are taken from the *Holy Bible, New Living Translation*, copyright © 1996, 2004, 2007 by Tyndale House Foundation. Used by permission of Tyndale House Publishers, Inc., Carol Stream, Illinois 60188. All rights reserved.

Scripture quotations marked NASB are taken from the *New American Standard Bible*®, Copyright © 1960, 1962, 1963, 1968, 1971, 1972, 1973, 1975, 1977, 1995 by The Lockman Foundation. Used by permission. (*www.Lockman.org*)

Scripture quotations marked NIV are taken from the Holy Bible, New International Version®, NIV®. Copyright © 1973, 1978, 1984, 2011 by Biblica, Inc.™ Used by permission of Zondervan. All rights reserved worldwide. www.zondervan.com. The "NIV" and "New International Version" are trademarks registered in the United States Patent and Trademark Office by Biblica, Inc.™

Scripture quotations marked THE MESSAGE are from *The Message*, copyright © by Eugene H. Peterson 1993, 1994, 1995. Used by permission of NavPress Publishing Group.

Edited by Bailey Utecht
Interior design: Design Corps
Cover design and illustration: Connie Gabbert Design and Illustration

Library of Congress Cataloging-in-Publication Data

Wise, Justin.
The social church : a theology of digital communication / Justin Wise.
  pages cm
Includes bibliographical references.
ISBN 978-0-8024-0987-4
1. Communication—Religious aspects—Christianity. 2. Digital communications.
3. Telecommunication. 4. Digital media—Religious aspects—Christianity. 5. Social media. I. Title.
BV652.95.W57 2014
261.5'2—dc23

                                                    2013036285

We hope you enjoy this book from Moody Publishers. Our goal is to provide high-quality, thought-provoking books and products that connect truth to your real needs and challenges. For more information on other books and products written and produced from a biblical perspective, go to *www.moodypublishers.com* or write to:

Moody Publishers
820 N. LaSalle Boulevard
Chicago, IL 60610

1 3 5 7 9 10 8 6 4 2

Printed in the United States of America

For my wife and children.
There are no greater joys in life than being
your husband and your dad.

CONTENTS

INTRODUCTION

I HAD AN ASTRONOMY professor in college (UNI Fight!) who sat us down on the first day of class and bluntly stated, "There's something you need to know about me." He continued as he scribbled on the chalkboard. "This is a 'u,' this is an 'r,' this is a 'v.'" He pointed to three letters that all looked exactly the same but were apparently not. "This is the only time I'm going to point this out this semester. I'm not going to take class time to clarify," he declared. "From now on, you'll need to figure it out for yourself. Now, on to the first lesson."

Personable, he wasn't. (For instance, he once publicly chided me for not knowing where Ursa Minor was in the school's planetarium. Hell hath no fury like an astronomy professor scorned by a constellation-challenged college freshman.) But he understood the need to set ground rules for proper learning to take place. Had he not coached us and given us a context for his (dreadful) penmanship, we would have been lost all semester—or at least questioned his intelligence. But given his instruction, most of us could figure out it was "planetary," not "planetavy." Context was, as they say, king.

You need to know a few things as we get started. Think of it as setting expectations. I like knowing we're on the same page, both literally and figuratively.

First, this is not a "how to" book. You will not learn how to set up a Facebook fan page or send your first tweet. You will not learn what Instagram is or how to use it. We're not going to look at how to use Pinterest for your church. You will not find the best times for updating your social networks, how to convince your senior pastor to blog, or what "the Google" is. (Don't laugh. I've had that question come up in several workshops I've led!) Those aren't bad things to learn, but there are many, many books, blogs, and articles covering the basics. This book will not be one of them.

Second, this book will not provide you simple answers. In fact, my hope is you close the book with more questions than when you started. Starting a Twitter account will not magically bring scores of young people through your church doors. "Engaging in the social media conversation" is a waste of time unless you understand why you're doing so. There are no copy-and-paste solutions. Hopefully, this book will surface questions your church has been unaware of (or worse, ignoring). My prayer is those questions will remain painfully present, like a splinter embedded under a fingernail.

What's needed now in the church is not "how to," but "where to." There is a significant gap between knowledge and application in the body of Christ surrounding social media. We're like a dog that's finally caught up to the car he's been chasing, then looks around quite listlessly asking the question, "Now what?"

Lastly, you're going to have to do some hard work to make this work. I don't want to sugarcoat it: translating who you are as a church into a digital communications strategy takes concerted effort by all levels of those involved with the organization. "We've always done it that way!" is more poisonous than ever. Innovation isn't just a virtue, it's a requirement. When communication patterns shift like they have in the last ten years, it's like shaking an Etch-a-Sketch after crafting an intricate design. All the hard work is gone, but the knowledge of how to create remains.

This book will help you discover your "why?" and answer the "now what?" that I see so many churches asking when confronted with the shift toward social. The people you will meet in this book will help fill the void between "know-how" and "do-now." As we'll see, we're facing one of the largest shifts in human communication in the history of the world. This is not hyperbole. Social media has caused literally every societal building block to adapt. Social media is a small, tip-of-the-iceberg, visible manifestation of the change we're facing: the gatekeepers are gone.

When this book goes to print, social media as we know it will be an inquisitive eight-year-old: just beginning to form an identity, but mostly a delightful little mess. We're all trying to figure this thing out. No one has the right answers. The box doesn't exist. The trail still needs to be blazed. The path remains unclear. This book will begin to provide you a way forward, but you will need to get your hands dirty. The question I need you to answer, dear reader, is will you join me?

THE WHY OF SOCIAL MEDIA

For God was in Christ, reconciling the world to himself,
no longer counting people's sins against them.
And he gave us this wonderful message of reconciliation.
So we are Christ's ambassadors; God is making his
appeal through us. We speak for Christ when we plead,
"Come back to God!"

2 CORINTHIANS 5:19–20

1

HERETICS NEEDED: APPLY WITHIN

IT WAS GETTING HOT up there on the podium. I could feel it. A prickly heat causing sweat to start trickling down the middle of my back.

I feared people in the crowd would notice I was both ultra-nervous and profusely perspiring. Of course, this worrying only added to my anxiety, which added to the sweating. I was starting to rethink my wardrobe choice that day: the lowly sweater vest.[1] (The sweater vest gets a bad rap, but it's both stylish and amazingly well-ventilated. But not on that day. It was holding in heat like a seat belt buckle in the sun.)

It was 2009, and I was presenting at the first ever Cultivate Conference, held at Park Community Church in Chicago, an event geared toward church communicators and creatives. I had spoken to crowds big and small, but for some reason this room was different. This crowd was different. The people in the room weren't there just to mindlessly absorb information; they were there to contribute. To help build and shape. There was a strong element of the unknown, and as the presenter, I knew I'd be going off-script soon and very soon. I'm comfortable with deviating from scheduled programming, but somehow I knew this experience would be unlike other workshops.

Here is how most of the conferences you and I attend transpire:

- A speaker, usually a white male, stands in front of the room.
- Speaker shares message, usually associated with their most recent book.
- Attendees sit for uncomfortably long periods of time in the same spot.
- Speaker leaves stage and the politely humorous emcee(s) distracts with giveaways, promotions, book releases . . . and MORE!
- Conference ends, we forget what was said one to three days later and go about our normal lives.

When Cultivate was in the planning stages, the creators wanted it to be different, and Cultivate was unique. How? For starters, the participants in the room could talk back. No more mindless consumption. Workshop sizes were purposefully kept small, no bigger than an elementary school class. Didn't understand a point the speaker made? Raise your hand and ask. Wanted to camp out on a particular point and explore an idea further? Pitch your tent and stay awhile. Cultivate created the space to freely interact. It was, most definitely, a two-way street.

My role as a workshop leader was more *discussion facilitator* than subject-matter expert, a pattern I wish more conferences would adopt. (The chances of being the one person in the room who knows more than anyone else are fool's odds.) At Cultivate, the audience was in control and they knew it.

What made this room so different was the size—no more than thirty people—and the nature of the talk. I couldn't just gloss over unclear ideas. Think of it as TED, but with the most brilliant minds on one subject converging in the same room. If you've ever spoken in public, you know there are times where a point you're making just isn't connecting—either with the audience or in your own mind—but you keep trudging forward. Cultivate exposed message confusion.

The message I shared at Cultivate was one I cared about deeply. The talk was called "What Would Luther Do?" It encapsulated everything I believed about where the church was headed and how we as leaders needed to face the changes in our congregations. In short, it focused on Martin Luther's efforts to widen the reach of the church using technology. As a life-long Lutheran, his story has always intrigued me. The more I dug into it, the more I realized Luther's narrative had real-time implications for some of the same changes and challenges the twenty-first century church is facing.

TUESDAYS WITH MARTY

In 1517, with a stein of beer and a fiery desire to see reform, a German monk named Martin Luther sat down to write. He wrote about the bothersome practices he saw in his local church. His focus narrowed on religious activities that betrayed the gospel message he had come to know intimately.

Church leaders during this period of history decided one of the best ways to fund the mission of the local church was to sell indulgences. The basic idea behind indulgences was simple: pay the church money, and one of your hell-bound relatives goes to heaven. A divine "get out of jail, free" card. You'd think I was joking, but sadly this is an all-too-real pit stop in the journey of the church.

In Luther's day there weren't denominations, per se. At least not in the sense you and I know them. There were the Eastern Orthodox folks (think "smells and bells"), the Moravians (liked to pray a lot, holed up on the side of a mountain), and the Roman Catholics. Roman Catholicism gave birth to Protestantism, thanks in part to Martin Luther and the rest of the Reformers, a group of individuals who wanted to see the church become all she was created to be.

Part of the impetus behind the Protestant movement was how the church dealt with indulgences. Luther, in short, wasn't down with it. He, along with many others, didn't see the connection between the gift of God's grace, freely available to all, and paying your way out of hell. The two seemed incompatible, and they were. Luther agreed deeply with St. Paul as he wrote, "For it is by grace you have been saved, through faith—and this is not from yourselves, it is the gift of God—*not by works, so that no one can boast*"[2] (emphasis mine). Those "works" included paying an amount—any amount—to the church to guarantee an existence with God in eternity. It is enough absurdity to even consider the logic of indulgences, but there were faithful men and women who clung to the false hope they offered. Johann Tetzel, a preacher and infamous spokesperson for indulgences, was fond of speaking to crowds and goading them to imagine a deceased family member trapped in purgatory.

His tagline was, "*So wie das Geld im Kasten klingt; die Seele aus dem Fegfeuer springt*" or "As soon as the gold in the casket rings; the rescued soul to heaven springs." Translated: you can buy your way into heaven. (Purgatory, by the way, is a supposed realm in the afterlife where some folks go after they die. Indulgences were supposed to help these unfortunate souls store up enough "merit" to finally move on up to their mansion in the sky.)

The lunacy behind indulgences was, of course, believing that God's grace could be bought. No repentance was required on behalf of the Christian. If one was feeling charitable, he or she could purchase an indulgence for dead Uncle Harry and hope it would finally tip the scales and dislodge their loved one from spiritual limbo.

This all prompted Luther to write about a new way of seeing reality in the church. A reality where all people—regardless of socioeconomic status—could live in relationship with God through Jesus Christ. No gatekeepers. No middle men. No negotiators. And most of all, no indulgences. Just Jesus. The church had lost its way, and Luther sought to clarify the popular theological thought of the day.

Luther believed everyone should have unfettered access to God. For forgiveness, yes, but most importantly, for relationship. Certainly this idea didn't originate with Luther, but his life's work seemed to hinge on this message. I imagine the words of the writer of Hebrews rang in his ears, "Let us come boldly to the throne of our gracious God."[3] In other words, *we don't need no stinking indulgences* (that's a rough translation, by the way). Followers of Jesus need not go through a mediator to receive grace; they had direct access to the place where grace flows from—the throne of God!

Not being one to rest on his stodgy laurels, Luther became a catalyst for the change he wanted to see. As mentioned, Luther began to write. Issues facing the church bubbled through his brain and pushed him to the edge of frustration. Indulgences were just a small part of the equation.

Luther's upbringing played a significant part in forming his theology. His father, Hans, was an exacting personality who pushed Luther to excel in all facets of life. But the pushing never stopped, and it led Luther to believe nothing he did was ever good enough. One need not be a psychiatrist to make the connection between Luther's relationship with his father and how his God paradigm was formed. A harsh, taskmaster father led him to believe, quite naturally, God behaved the same way. For Luther, indulgences were personal, as it pressed an already tender wound. A wound that told him, "You'll never be good enough for God."

The finished product of Luther's reformation writings was known as the "Ninety-Five Theses," a collection Luther publicly used to declare, "Things have got to change!" Not one for subversion and subtlety, he took his theses and literally nailed them to the door of the Castle Church of Wittenberg. It was a highly visible form of protest, the modern day equivalent of taking out a full-page ad in the *USA Today* that said something like:

> *Dear Pope,*
> *You're making some pretty serious mistakes.*
> *Cordially,*
> *Marty Luther*

Think about this for a moment. In the modern Western Christianity era, Bibles are readily available nearly everywhere. Entire bookstores are dedicated to them. Churches overflow with Bibles. Our iPhones, iPads, and mobile devices can access online versions of nearly every translation imaginable. You can't even stay in a hotel anymore where the Gideons haven't been first! (For the record, that's a good thing.)

Now imagine a culture where Bibles weren't ubiquitous. Imagine a society where Bibles were held under lock and key by the privileged few called "clergy." To have a Bible at your local church was considered a luxury. To have a Bible written in anything but Latin was virtually unheard of. The other problem? Most people didn't speak Latin. Like, not a word. Even if your church had access to Scripture, you had no idea what the priest was saying!

The first waves of reform crested when Luther began translating the Bible in 1521. He translated the whole canon of Scripture to common German. Then, in an act of measured defiance, he took the newly translated "Luther" Bible and sent it through the cutting-edge social technology of his day: the printing press.

It sounds strange to call the printing press "cutting-edge," but it was a technological marvel for its day. "History bears witness to the cataclysmic effect on society of inventions of new media for the transmission of information among persons . . . the development of printing [is an example]."[4] Writing moved from the scribe's desk to the printing press, and it changed *everything*. New ideas were able to travel across distances—both literal and figurative—previously perceived as unnavigable.

In Luther's case, what transpired next was nothing short of a miracle. For the first time, regular Germans (read: non-clergy) could read the Bible for themselves. Those who couldn't read (which were the majority of folks) could hear the Bible spoken in a language they could understand. Simply divine.

Luther's dream, aided by technology, became a vivid reality. He had done it. He bridged a widening gap between "us" (clergy) and "them" (laity). Boundaries were shattered and new stories could be written. All of this from a German monk with digestive problems. Who knew? Providence, it seems, is no respecter of persons. Perhaps this is what led Luther to declare the printing press was the "highest act of God's grace."[5]

WHAT WOULD LUTHER DO?

This story has always fascinated me. Maybe it's because I was raised Lutheran—baptized, first communion, confirmed, the whole bit. Potlucks, church coffee (which, described in a word, is gross), and liturgy. At times, we Lutherans have a tendency to idolize Luther to the point where, in some churches, he has more wall space than Jesus! Ol' Marty Luther certainly holds a special place in every Lutheran's heart.

This story resonates with me because it's a look at what a kingdom-minded person can accomplish with and through technology. By using the printing press to mass-produce the Bible, Luther set off a firestorm of reformation in the local church. Something needed to change, Luther felt the call, and he decided to do something about it. No waiting. No sitting around hoping someone would do it for him. Just a conviction and the confident assurance that God was with him. The printing press became an evangelistic tool in Luther's hands.

That was Luther's time. But what about our time? What stories have yet to be written for the twenty-first century church? What will our testimony be to the church universal? Will we seize the profound and unprecedented opportunity in front of us? Or will we allow the moment of innovation to pass? The church will never fail, but our methods might.

Becoming a social church means we need leaders who are willing to serve as heretics. Not theological heretics, mind you. I mean to say we need men and women who are willing to challenge long-standing and widely beloved methods of communicating the gospel message. People who are willing to bring some sacred cows to the barbecue and butcher them in front of everyone.

When describing a heretic, Seth Godin says in his book *Tribes*, "Heretics are engaged, passionate, and more powerful and happier than everyone else. . . . Heretics *must* believe. More than anyone else in an organization, it's the person who's challenging the status quo, the one who is daring to be great."[6]

I believe he's describing people like Jon Acuff, writer of the popular blog *Stuff Christians Like*. Jon rallied his readers to raise enough money to build not one, but two orphanages in Vietnam in the name of Jesus (that's $60,000 if you're keeping track[7]). This was all done without a church building, without a giving campaign, without a pastor quoting from Proverbs 3 or Deuteronomy 8. Just a man with a Spirit-breathed vision and a desire for change. No one gave him permission. He simply acted on faith and did something. In an age of budgets, committees, protocol, and church politics, this is heretical.

My friend Evelyn is a heretic. She's building a dance studio for young girls in one of the most heavily oppressed, patriarchal cultures on the face of the planet: Kabul, Afghanistan. Through the dance studio, she's inspiring a new generation of girls to think differently about themselves and what it means to be female. Social technology like Skype and email allow her to coordinate a team of overseers from literally around the globe. When it becomes safer to do so, she'll fund-raise for supplies and materials through the studio's website. Evelyn is heretical, in the best sense of the word.

Luther was a heretic. He was willing to stand for the change he wanted to see, regardless of the consequences. Whether it was persecution from church leaders, challenges from friends and colleagues, and, at times, his own crippling self-doubt, Luther stood against the common theological ideology of the day and said no. He leveraged social technology and pushed his message further and faster than it ever could have gone single-handedly or by word of mouth. We know the ending, so Luther's courage and vision easily get diminished. But he risked *everything*—sometimes unknowingly—to see his vision become reality.

Hearing these stories begs the question, "What would Luther do?" Thanks to the transition of broadcast to digital, and the pervasiveness of social media in nearly every facet of society, I can't help but wonder what Martin Luther's take would be.

Would social media be his new printing press? What might his Twitter feed look like? Would he have turned the Ninety-Five Theses into a flashy infographic? Blogged about the merits of infant baptism? Would his job title on LinkedIn be "Pastor, Reformer, Beer Drinker"? Maybe he would have configured a way to live stream his classes, giving access to all who wanted it. Either way, Luther would have been all over social media.

Church in the digital age necessarily requires heretics. The challenges and opportunities afforded by the advent of social media need to be addressed by men and women who see things differently, who aren't afraid to break rules. People who can embrace the "squishiness" and tension of the moment, and act.

I believe you're reading this book because you're a heretic. You see the power in social. You've experienced it firsthand. You've built new relationships, fortified existing ones, and seen the microcosm of your own world radically shift because of social technology. I believe your desire is to see the bride of Christ rise up and seize the opportunities in front of her. If that's you, you're in good company.

Much of what was discussed in this chapter was a direct extension of the conversation we had in the room at Cultivate. The ideas I brought to the room that resonated were built upon, changed, and improved. The ideas that fell flat remained there. While this certainly isn't a new way of presenting information

(Socratic method, anyone?), it's one that's suited for where our world—and the church—is heading.

This is what I appreciated about Cultivate. It was practically modeling a new way of "doing conferences" in a culture that demands to be heard. The organizers had their finger on the pulse of the values and thought processes of the real-world, flesh-and-blood culture just outside the doors of our churches, and they built a mechanism to reach it.

The world is waiting for the church to rise up in the digital era. Leaders and heretics are needed. The question we'll answer together is this: What does it look like to be the Social Church?

2

CALCULATED RULE—BREAKING

HAVE YOU EVER HAD a defining moment in your life that God used to shape your vision, dreams, and hopes for the future? Snapshots in time that crystalize to form the narrative of who you are as a person? Moments your senses seem to remember the same way a glove remembers the shape of your hand?

One of those paradigm-creating moments for me came in 2008. I was on staff at Lutheran Church of Hope in West Des Moines, Iowa. My role at the church bounced from intern to discipleship coordinator to college ministry leader and finally landed on "digital director." None of us knew exactly what that meant, but it sounded cool and it meant I got to play around on social media all day.

Part of my self-directed responsibilities meant I needed to get the church on Facebook. I had seen a number of churches use Facebook effectively in creating an online community, providing the congregation with important announcements and information, and providing a space for members to connect with one another throughout the week.

It's commonplace now for churches to be on social networks like Facebook. But back in 2008 this was still a relatively new practice. Many churches were still in the exploratory phase, asking questions like, "Should we be using social media?" The question has since been answered ("yes," if you're wondering), but I had seen enough positive examples to know my church needed to be in this space. For better or worse, I wanted us to be pioneers in this area—and coming from a Lutheran church, that's saying something!

The sticky part in all of this was my senior pastor's sentiment toward social media. To put it plainly, he hated it. "Hate" may be overstating it, although not by much. One thing was for sure: his position wasn't neutral!

Like many leaders, his main concern was opening up the church and its staff to unwarranted criticism of any kind. With good reason, too. At the time, our church was just less than 10,000 members, which meant there were a lot of opinions floating around! For Pastor Mike, the risk wasn't worth the reward, which made my decision to dip the collective toes of our church into the social media waters even more risky.

I knew I was breaking an unwritten rule, but I did it anyway. In starting a Facebook fan page for my church, I was aware I hadn't been given expressed permission to do so. I also knew, in my own defense, I hadn't been told to *not* create one either. "Better to ask forgiveness than permission," as the saying goes.

After starting the under-the-radar fan page, momentum began to grow. Quickly. Much quicker than I was anticipating. In less than a month we had close to 2,000 fans. When you have a congregation the size of Lutheran Church of Hope's, getting those kinds of numbers happens automatically. I had done zero promotion of the page, but when word got out, it grew like the weeds in my backyard vegetable garden. People found out quickly, and when they did, they wanted to be a part of the community.

I started having some serious reservations about my decision to put the church online. Not because it wasn't working, but because it was! You have to understand, this decision was much bigger than just starting a page on Facebook. It represented a new way of relating to our congregation, our community . . . the world!

REAL MINISTRY IN THE RISK

For many, many years, churches communicated in the same fashion you and I drive down a one-way street: traffic only moved one way. When a church had something to say (*Bake sale! New worship service! Potluck!*), they found the appropriate channel to broadcast the message (mailing postcard, bulletin, announcements, etc.), and then sent the message. The expectation was there was no expectation. Churches broadcasted a message and never anticipated a moment where the congregation would start speaking back. Message out, silence in return—like the radio signals sent out into space in hopes of reaching intelligent life.

But social media has changed this dynamic. In a scene of the movie *Contact*, Jodie Foster's character says, "If it's just us [humans], it seems like an awful waste of space." The radio signals found intelligent life, and it started speaking back. For the church, and virtually every other sector of society, the shift to social permanently turned the tables in the public's favor. Social media gave people a voice, and they're not going to give it up easily.

I knew this momentum shift meant that, sooner or later, Mike was going to find out about the Facebook page. I didn't want him to discover it by accident. I knew I had to be the one to tell him, but given his predisposition toward social media, I didn't know how the conversation was going to go. He could either be thrilled by my initiative or frustrated by my rule-bending.

I'm happy to report he was very much in the former category. In fact, when I showed him the activity on the fan page—the church members encouraging each other, the Scripture being shared, and the events being promoted—he stepped back and said something I'll never forget: "There's real ministry happening here!" He saw the way the body of Christ was growing, connecting, and encouraging one another—real, practical ways people were growing in their faith—and rightly called it a holy moment.

I couldn't help but think about St. Peter in Acts, watching God touch the lives of those previously believed to be untouchable.[1] How big of a mind-shift it must have been for Peter to see God shattering boundaries in place for as long as he, and most of his ancestors, could remember. But Peter was quick to recognize the best thing to do when God moves is to get out of the way and ask, "How can I be a part of this?" It didn't take Peter long to let God transform his entire way of thinking; the "outsiders" quickly became part of the family.

Pastor Mike recognized the weight of what was happening online that day and, like Peter, let God change his mind almost immediately. I believe his mind-shift was so distinct and immediate because, being a faithful man sensitive to God's Spirit, he perceived the potential of what a church online could do. No more boundaries, no more borders, no more physical limitations for God's Word going forth. Anyone with an Internet connection could be a part of the church universal with the click of a mouse.

It was in that moment I sensed a deeply personal call on my life to help churches build God's kingdom online. My interaction with Mike that day left an imprint on my soul that said, "Ministry can happen online . . . you get to show them how!" It was a clear moment I heard God speaking to me. Not audibly, but a moment I knew what his plan was for me and what he was asking me to do. I don't know if you've ever experienced something like this, but the confidence that stems from a God-call is nearly unquenchable.

The power of a church online goes way beyond a simple social network like Facebook. As you'll hear me say often throughout this book, social networks will come and go. If you're reading this book ten years from now (2024, baby!), Facebook, Twitter, and YouTube may be a distant memory. By then, social networks will probably be hardwired into our brains or something. (As the young Elijah Wood said in the classic *Back to the Future Part II* while playing a "retro" video arcade game from the 1980s, "Aw, man! You mean you have to use your hands?"[2]) The underlying power in social media is not the technology. It's the power that comes from human beings connecting from all around the globe.

If the gospel message (or any message, for that matter) is transmitted along relational lines, churches can confidently head in the direction of social because of the volume of relationships it can facilitate. Pastor Mike and I talked a few weeks after the "Facebook reveal," and he remarked how easy it was to wish people happy birthday. This may seem incidental, but when a pastor of a 10,000+ church can personally wish congregation members to have a great birthday, the relationship is fortified.

Some of you reading this book need to consider what calculated rule-breaking looks like in your context. Not outright disobedience, but an allegiance to a call that supersedes the bureaucracy getting in your way. I even hesitate to write this, but some of you may need to break the rules to get the breakthrough your church needs. Are you prepared to make this decision?

Certainly don't make any decisions for calculated rule-breaking in a vacuum. Discuss with those around you who you trust. Keep in mind that breaking rules for the sake of breaking them is, at best, obnoxious, and at worst, destructive. But as a friend of mine is fond of saying, "It's more fun to be a pirate on a ship than jump overboard." Realize there may come a moment when you decide the consequences of not acting are greater than the consequences of your actions.

The power of calculated rule-breaking comes in the new reality your decision creates. Once you move in a direction, it begins to unfold a whole new realm of exciting possibilities and realities that didn't exist before. Catalyzed by your decision, these realities—say, community forming on a Facebook page or orphanages being built in Vietnam—become harder to deny. Ideas and theories are easy to dismiss because they exist in the ether.

But when you take an idea and put it into motion, it begins to form an identity all its own. The shape and form may look different from what you anticipated, but that's to be expected. The fact you took action means you have something to point to and say, "Here, look. We must deal with this now."

When Nirvan Mullick set out to create a documentary about a nine-year-old boy's cardboard arcade, he probably wasn't thinking of how to create the next viral social media sensation. And yet, that's exactly what happened. Mullick's film, *Caine's Arcade*, became an exercise in calculated rule-breaking that catalyzed a movement of "cardboard creativity & play around the world."[3] As you might have guessed, the movement was greatly facilitated when the film went viral, racking up more than 7 million views on YouTube and Vimeo.

Or take my friend Kevin. He was facing the difficult task at his software development job of communicating the value of social media to his senior leadership team. His leaders weren't antagonistic to the change, but they weren't ready to embrace it either. Instead of fussing, fighting, and pouting about how no one listened to him, Kevin commandeered two of his friends in the department and built, from scratch, a social networking prototype app for the business. (The app demonstrated how social media could help increase revenue for the company.) No one told him to do this; he just did it. The working model took about two weeks of nights and weekends to build, but when he showed it to his superiors, they quickly jumped on board. The app did what no amount of persuading could do, all because he took a calculated risk.

My friend Brian persuaded his church to stop wasting (*lots*) of money on pricey billboards and direct mailers by doing a side-by-side experiment with Facebook ads. For one month, he took a small portion of his allotted "billboard budget," and put it toward ads on Facebook that carried the same messages as the billboards. I'll spare you the gory details, but the Facebook ads were 400 percent more effective than the billboards at achieving agreed upon results. Again, no asking, just action.

The point is simple: churches need leaders who will take a risk and break the stranglehold of "this is how it's always been." There is too much at stake. Local congregations who don't make the transition, those who refuse to turn the corner, will most likely see their influence fade and, eventually, disappear. Those who choose to carefully break the established rules, those who adapt, will survive.

3

CAVE WALLS, MARTIANS, AND THE HISTORY OF COMMUNICATION

WE ARE LITERALLY HARD-WIRED to communicate. It's in our blood. We can't help ourselves. It's at the core of who we are.

In ancient times, the simplest and most readily available form of technology was spoken language, and our histories were kept alive through oral tradition. Stories were repeated and memorized, passed down from generation to generation. Messages that needed to be sent across miles were carried in the minds of runners.

It may come as a surprise, but the culture we see in both the Old and New Testaments were largely oral cultures. The earliest gospel account, for instance, was Matthew[1], and it was written somewhere between AD 50 and AD 70. If you're keeping track, this is *decades* after the ministry of Jesus. For our modern minds, this gives us pause. We might think, "What took so long?" We tweet, text, and blog about experiences as they happen. Why would the gospel writers allow so much time to pass between the resurrection of Jesus and the time they started documenting his story?

For starters, their societal communication patterns were much different than ours. Being an orally based culture, it didn't occur to the gospel writers to document what they experienced in Dragnet style ("Just the facts, ma'am"). It would be like going back in time to 1990 and asking a friend to text you their dinner plans for the night. They wouldn't have any idea what you were talking about! To have the earliest accounts of Jesus' life appear a few short decades after he died is the modern-day equivalent of breaking news. It was screamingly fast, and we can't criticize the writers of Scripture for dragging their feet by our modern standards.

Nonetheless, the Bible is a written account of God's interaction with human beings at various points in history. It should be noted, writing and literacy are interlinked, as one is not possible without the other. Broadly speaking, societal literacy rates throughout history have almost always favored the educated, and therefore *wealthy*, individuals of a given culture. One need not look any further than the New Testament itself. Matthew was a (presumably wealthy) tax collector; Luke was a doctor; and Paul, the man responsible for nearly two-thirds of the New Testament, was a "Hebrew's Hebrew" and a Roman citizen, the modern equivalent of Kobe Bryant being knighted by the queen of England herself. To write was to have power.

More broadly speaking, the history of written communication is murky, as human beings have been carving messages into cave walls since our earliest ancestors roamed the earth. But through written language, as we know it, a new era was born. History could be documented, scribed in books and scrolled on leaves of papyrus. As more people became literate, knowledge and information could be passed more easily and quickly. Messages could be posted in public, or private letters could be sent.

As we've seen, the high point of this technology came with the invention of the printing press in 1440. Historians should take note that the first book printed was the Bible.

THE POWER OF BROADCAST

The next major change occurred in the twentieth century with the invention of broadcasting. Now, a single message could reach thousands, even millions, of people all over the world simultaneously, which helped to create a popular, or mass culture.

This mode of communication, I think, can best be typified by the response of the American public when Orson Welles broadcasted his now infamous radio adaptation of H. G. Wells's literary work *The War of the Worlds* on CBS radio in 1938.

Millions heard the radio broadcast. It was themed as a mock breaking-news bulletin informing the public that Martians had landed on Earth. Of course, no Martians had actually invaded the planet, but judging by the public's reaction, one would be led to believe much differently.

To put it plainly, people *freaked*. Mass hysteria broke out. Pandemonium ensued with people running out of their homes into the streets, screaming, packing up their cars, and heading for the hills. People in the 1930s would listen to the radio in the same way we watch television, gathered around the set listening to news updates, music programs, and sports broadcasts. To have a message of this magnitude interrupt a medium in its infancy was a big deal. To say the public had a blind trust in the media would be doing a disservice to their collective intelligence. Perhaps it would be better to say they simply had no reason to distrust what they were hearing.

Orson Welles gave them a reason to be skeptical. Here's a portion of the broadcast:

> Ladies and gentlemen, this is the most terrifying thing I have ever witnessed. . . . Wait a minute! Someone's crawling out of the hollow top. Someone or . . . something. I can see peering out of that black hole two luminous disks . . . are they eyes? It might be a face. It might be . . . Good heavens, something's wriggling out of the shadow like a gray snake. Now it's another one, and another. They look like tentacles to me. There, I can see the thing's body. It's large as a bear and it glistens like wet leather. But that face, it . . . Ladies and gentlemen, it's indescribable. I can hardly force myself to keep looking at it. The eyes are black and gleam like a serpent. The mouth is kind of V-shaped with saliva dripping from its rimless lips that seem to quiver and pulsate.[2]

How terrifying! Can you imagine hearing this live, for the first time? The radio, in those days, was seen as a trusted friend. It was a link to the outside world—informing you of what was happening, with whom, and for how long. It gave you eyes to see the world and shaped the popular culture of the day. Welles's "news bulletin" lasted only a few brief moments, but it frayed the collective nerves of a nation and, I believe, permanently altered its psyche.

The "War of the Worlds" episode serves as a metaphor for the sheer power of the broadcast era of communication. Orson Welles manufactured national mass hysteria with little more than a microphone, a few voice actors, and a production studio. The decisive factor was having the power of a national broadcasting powerhouse—CBS—whose tentacles reached into millions of American homes nationwide. This made all the difference.

Welles would not have been able to achieve the same effect with print—at least, not with the scale, scope, and immediacy national broadcast radio provided.

The "War of the Worlds" news flash perfectly encapsulates the allure of the broadcast era of human communication. One person, company, or organization—one *source*—held the means to communicate one message to many people. One-to-many. As Biola University professor David Bourgeois writes:

> At the turn of the twentieth century, we were yet again introduced to a new communication breakthrough. Unlike the telegraph (and its followup, the telephone), which had to be connected via a wire and only allowed point-to-point communication, allowed one person to reach many locations at the same time. This new "broadcast" technology allowed us to be in multiple places at once.[3]

Broadcast gave us unheralded opportunities to see and hear the weaving of our cultural fabric as it happened. The *Hindenburg* disaster, Lou Gehrig's final address, Hitler's declaration of war, the first televised presidential debate between Nixon and Kennedy, Martin Luther King Jr.'s "I Have a Dream" speech, human beings landing on the moon—the impact of these historical events were magnified by the power of broadcast technology. What happened in one part of the world may have been relegated to the sometimes cold, two-dimensional world of print had it not been for radio and television.

But all of those events—along with millions more—were given a *weight* they may not have had otherwise. It is one thing to read about a man being shot; it is quite another to see the shaky footage of the assassination of President John F. Kennedy, captured by Abraham Zapruder. One can read about the liberation of a people group from the clutches of Communism, but it is another thing to actually see the Berlin Wall crumbling to its foundations. These events took place in a finite location (Dallas, Texas, and Berlin respectively), but we witnessed them from the four corners of the globe—both as they happened and decades later.

The weight of this makes me nostalgic for broadcast technology to have been present at other moments in history. How I would have loved to both see and hear Abraham Lincoln deliver his renowned Gettysburg Address. Or hear the sound of Martin Luther's voice. Or listen to Joan of Arc exclaim, "I was born for this."[4] How differently we might view the American Civil War if, like in Operation Desert Storm, we could have seen the bombs soaring through the night sky, exploding on their intended targets. These events, as we know, are sealed off from the reaches of history. We experience them now only through the printed word, paintings, and black-and-white photos.

However, it is the "one person, many locations" mantra that became the broadcast era's biggest strength and ultimately its largest weakness. As the saying goes, "Absolute power corrupts absolutely." Broadcasting brought an immense amount of power to whoever had the means to control it. Its heroes were Walter Cronkite, Ronald Reagan, Ed Sullivan, and Johnny Carson.

Just as broadcast brought us world-changing moments like those listed earlier, it has also brought us pain, distortion, and darkness. The Flintstones—everyone's favorite prehistoric animated family—were used to sell cigarettes in the 1950s. The "Dune effect," using broadcast media to manipulate public opinion by disseminating war-time propaganda. Desensitizing a culture to violence, the average eighteen-year-old has seen 200,000 violent actions committed on television over the course of his life, including 40,000 murders.[5] Jersey Shore (that's all I need to say).

Many of you reading this book grew up (or had parents who grew up) in the broadcast era. This method of communication comes embedded with its own set of values; however, exploring them would be outside the scope of this book. Suffice it to say, broadcast reflects many of the same values of the Industrial Revolution, namely "consumption."

> Where thrift, savings, and staying out of debt were once thought to be fundamental virtues, after the Industrial Revolution, consumption, consumption, consumption became the watchwords. If too few people purchased the rapidly expanding array of goods, store shelves would never empty, factory orders would fall, and people would be laid off as factories closed. The only way to stave off economic ruin was to re-educate the population to become intensive consumers, buying many things they would never have imagined before.[6]

It was broadcast technology that was almost solely responsible for the "re-education" of the population. If you've ever wondered why your grandmother saves and washes her plastic sandwich bags like mine does, it's because she (and many others from her generation) did not believe in waste. To go into debt, for anything, was seen as a mark of shame to be avoided at all costs. With average American household credit card debt weighing in at more than $15,000,[7] we've clearly left these values behind, and we have the broadcast era to thank for it.

Broadcast technology allowed the industry known as "advertising" to evolve for the purpose of selling people things they didn't need, to fund companies (and executives) who didn't care about the people they sold things to. Anything to keep the machine going! Even if the "anything" was crushing consumer debt.

SIMUL JUSTUS ET PECCATOR

The technology, however, was not the problem. How we chose to use it was the problem. Technology is amoral in the sense it is like a brick. A brick is neither inherently "bad" nor "good." It does not possess moral qualities. But a brick can be used for harm or benefit. For instance, throwing a brick through a neighbor's window would be harmful. Someone could get hurt or cut by the glass, and your neighbor will have to spend money to replace it. Conversely, using a brick to start building a home for a family in need would be beneficial for them. They would have a warm place to stay, gain a sense of dignity, and provide a safe place for the children to live in.

The presence of technology is amoral. Communication technology can be used to benefit us—reuniting long lost childhood friends on Facebook, connecting people in need of an organ transplant to donors, donating money online to a worthy cause, or seeing the ripples of a Baptist preacher telling the world, "I have a dream . . ." As we've seen, communication technology can also be used to harm us—online bullying, sexual harassment through disposable media apps like Snapchat, child pornography, and intentionally manipulating the minds of the general public for financial gain.

As followers of Jesus, we know from where this struggle emanates, don't we? We know we are a plagued people, simultaneously capable of scaling the highest heights and dredging the lowest lows. We offer the change in our pockets to the homeless who line our streets, yet we greedily protest the measures put into place to ensure those same people have a chance of getting off the streets. We live in a post-civil rights country, where equality is to be the law of the land. Yet our Sunday morning services still remain one of the most segregated hours in America. We are the ones who cry "Hosanna!" and the ones who shout "Crucify him!" As Luther once stated, we are *simul justus et peccator*—both sinner and saint, all in the same being.[8] Is it any wonder our sinful nature creeps into our communication methods?

CONFUSING THE LANGUAGE

In Genesis 11, we read the story of Babel. Most of us are familiar with it, but it bears repeating here because of the theological importance of communication. Back in the day, everyone spoke the same language. With more than 7,000 active languages being spoken across the world today,[9] it's hard to imagine everyone being on the same linguistic page. But this was the case and it created an incredible amount of synergy. As God himself said, "Nothing they set out to do will be impossible for them!"[10]

The folks of Babel decided it would be helpful to build a tower, or *stairway*, to heaven. "We can build anything!" they said. "Let's go take a look around and see what God is up to!" God, being God, saw right through their plan and turned Babel into the customs gate at La Guardia—dozens of different dialects, all chatting away. We were no longer of one accord, mainly because we couldn't understand one another. We no longer spoke the same language. Like a high school house party after the cops show up, we scattered.

It's important to note God's rationale behind confusing the language of the people. One might read this passage and think, "Why would God do something like that?" I can understand, as it sounds peculiar for him to be *against* unity amongst his people. But there's more to the story.

I liken it to the time my son was building an actual tower with couch cushions, stuffed animals, and anything else he could find in the middle of our living room. My wife was out on errands and, well, I let him build his tower a little bit higher than I should. The process culminated with my three-year-old son hurling his tiny, thirty-eight-pound body from the couch armrest onto his haphazardly assembled tower, tumbling head-over-feet down to the floor. I don't know if you've ever had the sensation of feeling your heart catapult out of your chest, but this experience did it for me. "My gosh," I thought, "I broke him!" Thankfully, he popped right back up and said, "Again!" while starting to build another tower. I needed to step in and stop the process before he actually got hurt. A three-year-old doesn't understand things like compound fractures, broken arms, and upset mommies.

In Genesis 11, God saw a people who mistakenly took success as invincibility. They had succeeded in not only building their society, but they had navigated the choppy waters of human relationships and excelled. If there is such a thing as Utopia, this was it. But God stepped in and said, "Not so fast, gang." The sin in the Tower of Babel wasn't the use of technology (their man-made building materials) or being of one accord (the Bible is decidedly pro-unity amongst humans). The sin occurred when "The people of Babel saw technology as the means by which they could overcome the limits of a sinful world and remain independent of God."[11] That, as they say, will preach.

Our sin knows no bounds. It affects us spiritually, mentally, emotionally, and in the ways we communicate with one another. The technology we create can be used for good and for evil. That which we create to serve us ends up ruling us. This has never been truer than in the case of broadcast technology.

THE WWW

But like all good things ("good" being a subjective term here), the broadcast era had to come to an end. During the end of the twentieth century, society began transitioning from broadcast communication to the digital era. The big media conglomerates who held the means to broadcast a message—be it the Berlin Wall coming down, Neil Armstrong landing on the moon, or what dryer sheets you should be using—saw their power dwindle with the emergence of the Internet.

The Internet allowed the "few" to become "many." Unlike broadcast technology, no single person or organization held the means for message dissemination. ABC, CBS, and NBC gave way to HTTP, URL, and DSL. Communication became a two-way street between the "haves" and the "have-nots." Yes, multi-billion dollar businesses like Google, Facebook, and Twitter have emerged during this era. One could even make the case that the giants somehow "control" the Internet, controlling the same editorial decisions as the broadcast that titans of yesteryear used to make.

The main difference, of course, is openness. The Internet allows anyone with the desire to start a blog, a Facebook page, or an online video channel, in most cases for no charge. These Internet-based communication channels have the potential to reach the same amount of people, yet (as of this writing) there is little to no regulation around them. As we keep hearing, the Internet is like the wild, wild West.

The same cannot be said about broadcast communication. You and I can't waltz down to our local news station and ask to have unrestricted air time, for little to no charge, to say and express whatever views we'd like. It doesn't work like that. For starters, broadcast doesn't scale in the same way digital does. Second, those who own the means of communication have built very profitable businesses using those means and have no intention of giving them up freely. Third, and as a reminder, broadcast serves "one to many," not the "many to many" the Internet so freely provides.

In this cauldron of communication, social media was born. In many ways "social media" is a misnomer because, as we'll see later, media has always been social. But if the Internet is the mother of digital communication, social media are her somewhat tempestuous children. FriendFeed, MySpace, Facebook, Google+, Pinterest, Friendster, Twitter, YouTube (and many, many more)—some of them are still with us, some of them are not. But each one of these networks represents the idea that people have a voice and this voice can be shared with the world—for better or worse!

In the transition to the digital era, social media are transforming the basic building blocks of our society. You can ask the president of the United States questions on Reddit.com . . . and he'll actually respond. Purchases are influenced by ratings, friends, and family members rather than ads, endorsements, and commercials. Complete courses from MIT and Harvard can be accessed online and for no cost. (If you have a question, you can tweet the professors, too.) The way we relate to one another is changing. The digital media revolution means that, as new media legend Gary Vaynerchuck is fond of saying, "The gatekeepers are gone."

It would be foolish to think that faith-based communities are immune from social's reach. The local church is an organization. Organizations are filled with people. People communicate. When the way people communicate with each other changes, the organization will change. This process is happening in megachurches, house churches, and everything in between. It's affecting young and old congregations, mainline and evangelical churches, emergent and conservative churches. No one is immune. When the gatekeepers disappear, everyone is affected. The church is no different.

Seth Godin writes on his blog, "The newspaper business, the steel business, law firms, the car business, the record business, even computers . . . one by one, our industries are being turned upside down, and so quickly that it requires us to change faster than we'd like."[12] We all feel this tension, don't we? We all sense it happening intuitively.

I see it in the concerned look on the face of pastors when I speak at conferences or work with churches. They seemed dazed, like after taking a right-cross from Manny Pacquiao. They ask questions like, "How do we control the conversation on our Facebook page?" and "How do we make sure no one on staff says something inappropriate on social media?" The answer to both questions is, of course, you can't. You cannot control the online conversation surrounding your church, business, or organization. You can only take steps to influence it.

Social requires action. There is a certain level of proactivity churches must adopt as the digital era dawns on us. Some churches will heed the call and move forward. Others, sadly, will not and they will not survive. You may think this is an overstatement, but the data shows something much different. For instance, the Evangelical Lutheran Church in America (ELCA), the largest Lutheran denomination in the world, had a nearly 25 percent decrease in membership since 1987.[13] The two biggest years of decline came in 2010 and 2011. Construction spending on religious institutions is plummeting, and has been since 2002.[14] The Southern Baptist Convention (SBC) has not grown in membership since 2006, and the trend is decidedly continuing.[15]

While these trends cannot directly be traced to social media adoption failure, I do believe they stem from the church's inability (maybe even unwillingness?) to speak the language of the culture that surrounds it.

At this point, some of you might be tempted to say, "That may be the case in other churches, but not here!" I understand that change can be scary. Terrifying even. It may truly be that in your immediate context, social hasn't emerged as prominently as it has in other churches. There is a possibility, you may just not be aware of it. This is not meant to condemn or judge, as these changes are hard. I sincerely hope seeing these facts provides a wake-up call for those who may still be in denial.

Either way, the trends around social show skyrocketing adoption rates with no indication of slowing down. There is a 91 percent adoption rate of social networking amongst American adults ages eighteen to thirty-four.[16] The average Internet user is spending 4.6 hours on social networks per week,[17] more than any other category. And do you know the fastest growing Facebook user segment? Retirees over 65.[18] Grandma has got to see her grandkids!

The question isn't, "Is social media here to stay?" The answer is in. It's a resounding yes! The social networks we use will continue to be a revolving door (remember Ping? FriendFeed? Google Buzz?), but the essence of the social shift (interactivity, ubiquity, deep personalization, always-connected, mobile first) is here to stay.

Religious leaders everywhere need to consider what a social church looks like. When social networks can help topple dictators in heavily oppressed countries like Egypt and Libya, build orphanages for children in Vietnam, and mobilize literally thousands, maybe millions, of people at a moment's notice, any smart person with a message should be paying attention. As I think we'd all agree, the church has a very important message.

The real question is, "*How* can the church become more social?" How can we become a community-based organization that intentionally seeks to make its cause more accessible? How can we embrace the changes brought on by social media rather than sticking our collective head in the ground, pretending they don't exist? How can we use social to tear down the wall between "us" and "them," whoever "them" might be in our given contexts (e.g., young people, older people, the gay and lesbian community, people of color)?

You'll meet churches and leaders in this book who have embraced these changes and plotted a course forward with courage and vision. People like Johanna Price of Eagle Brook Church located in the Twin Cities. For any major event in the church, Johanna and her team build a social media component into their communication strategy, just as they would for print materials or verbal announcements. You'll meet people like Scott Ballard of The Village Church in Dallas. Scott said to me recently regarding the church's social networks, "I want as many people as possible to have access to our resources so the gospel can go forth and lives be changed." These are the words of someone who, like Luther, understands the power of the technology within his grasp.

Ultimately this is where the value of social media lies—in its ability to use technology to facilitate connection and relationships between real people. Emerging generations see little to no difference between an "online" and "offline" world. They are becoming one in the same. If half of the world's population is under thirty, ambassadors of the gospel message need to understand the preferences, patterns, behaviors, and values of the people living in a twenty-first century world.

Throughout every major communication shift in history, people of faith have been at the forefront of change. Whether it was Luther and the printing press, Aimee Semple McPherson and the radio broadcast, or Billy Graham and his televangelist crusades, Jesus people have seized the opportunity placed in front of them for the sake of the kingdom. The history books remain unwritten for the digital era. The pages are blank. What will your contribution be? Quoting from Joshua, in both words and sentiment, "As for me and my family, we will serve the Lord!"[19]

THE EMBEDDED VALUES OF A NEW MEDIA CULTURE

From the tribe of Issachar, there were 200 leaders of the tribe with their relatives. All these men understood the signs of the times and knew the best course for Israel to take.

1 CHRONICLES 12:32

4

SIGNS OF THE TIMES

I REMEMBER THE FIRST time I heard Cynthia Ware speak. Having been familiar with Cynthia's writings on her blog, *Digital Sanctuary*, I was eager to hear her speak in person. It was 2008, and I had just logged on to watch the live stream of Church TechCamp from my office at the church I was working at in Des Moines. The TechCamp was described as a "localized unconference for people of faith to gather and share their own best practices"[1] from the field of digital ministry. This "unconference" was taking place in Pasadena, California, but through the magic of live streaming was beaming live to the four corners of the globe to anyone with an Internet connection.

Nowadays streaming live events are commonplace, but back in 2008, this was still a relatively new idea, which enticed me even more. My job at the time was serving in a young professionals/college ministry, but I had a growing interest in the developing discipline of digital ministry. Most of the people I interacted with on a daily basis were using digital media to stay in touch with each other throughout the day. Facebook, Twitter, email, texting—if it was digital, they were all over it! (By the way, I've never felt quite right with the term "young people," especially since I wasn't much older than most of the folks I was leading in my ministry!)

Cynthia was slated to speak, along with several others, but she was one of the main reasons I logged on and tuned in. I knew Cynthia had an actual degree in new media technologies. (If you're wondering what "new media" is, it's what they called social media before it hit the main cultural vein.) She was studying the effects of relational media well before it took root in the life of the church. Much like Neil Postman in his work *Amusing Ourselves to Death*, I saw Cynthia as a digital prophetess, speaking on the direction the church needed to go digitally. In many ways, she was (and still is) very much ahead of her time.

Cynthia kicked things off and took the "stage." I say stage, but it was just a classroom at Fuller Seminary. The lighting was bad, the audio cut in and out, and every so often, the face of John Saddington (of 8BIT fame) would fill the screen as he made necessary camera adjustments.

It didn't matter, though. The focus of the event wasn't the setting, it was the ideas. The main idea being ministry can happen online and we, as the church, have an obligation to understand how. If businesses, nonprofits, and educational institutions were making the necessary investments to understand online communication, how much more should the church? Church Tech-Camp aimed to answer this question through short talks given by thought leaders like Cynthia.

As she stepped up to speak, she quoted from 1 Chronicles 12, verse 32:

> From the tribe of Issachar, there were 200 leaders of the tribe with their relatives. *All these men understood the signs of the times and knew the best course for Israel to take.* (emphasis mine)

Hearing those words changed the course of my life. That may sound like hyperbole, but it's not. Outside of seminary, I could not remember an Old Testament text being used so profoundly as to affect the way I lived my life. I've always had a soft spot for the Old Testament, mainly because it's just so very *odd*. Additionally, our churches have been indoctrinated with the subtle lie that the Old Testament is somehow the vestigial organ of Scripture. As a seminary professor of mine was fond of saying, "The OT is not short for 'the Optional Testament.'" ZING!

In the original context of the Issachar text, it's talking about the leaders of a group of people who followed God. These groups, or tribes, were special because God—or Yahweh—called them out and said, "You guys are really something special. I want to show you how the world works. Just walk with me, pay attention, and everything will be just fine." Part of that walk included giving each tribal leader a specific skill; most had to do with bravery, weaponry, or an ability related to battle.

The leaders from the tribe of Issachar were different. They had a God-given ability to sense and discern what was going on in the world around them and determine next steps for all the tribes. The Issachar leaders knew intuitively the right thing to do. You can imagine how incredibly useful this would be. Although Scripture never references specifically *how* they used this gifting, I imagine it looked like being able to step back and see the big picture. When everyone else was myopically focused on the one or two steps in front of them, wondering whose heads they could chop off next, the group from Issachar could see miles on down the road. Temporary setbacks didn't rattle them. They saw the potential of where God's call on their lives could take them. For the leaders of Issachar, it wasn't a matter of *if*, but *when*.

We know people like this, don't we? Men and women in our lives who possess a unique ability, a knack, for charting the right course. We may call them "mentors" or "teachers," but we go to these individuals when we have a question or problem that needs sorting out. They have a vantage point that enables them to point out the multiple threads converging in our lives at any given moment.

If you've had the pleasure of having someone like this in your life, you know how uncanny it can be. What we see in black and white, they see in three dimensions. As a friend once said of his mentor, "It's like he's been reading my mail!" Yes, if the postal service existed back then, I imagine the leaders from Issachar would have been accused of reading other Israelites' mail on more than one occasion!

This was the gist of Cynthia's talk. A rousing charge challenging us to become the visionary leaders like the ones from the tribe of Issachar. We, as next generation leaders tackling the relatively unknown field of digital ministry, needed the ability to see further down the road if we were to be effective in our ministry settings. Being a "visionary" leader was no longer an option. She began to unpack the notion that our world was literally changing faster than we had ability to comprehend. The onset of digital communication was putting everything into hyperdrive—commerce, government, education, and yes, even faith. We were being required to make decisions faster than ever before because the speed at which we communicate was rapidly increasing. For someone who has always enjoyed studying the way people communicate, her words riveted me from the very start.

GENERATIONAL MEDIA VALUES

Cynthia transitioned into unpacking the embedded values of a new media culture. These values—interactivity, sharing, personalization, ubiquity, and connectedness—shape the

decision-making and thought process of an entire digital generation. While no one can hold a candle to the depth of knowledge
Cynthia brings to the table on this subject, I want to unpack
these embedded new media values with the hope of contextualiz-
ing the rest of this book. Simply put, this is how a digital culture
thinks.

First, it is important to understand how different generations
approach new media. (By the way, I use the terms "new media,"
"social media," and "digital communication" synonymously. They
all represent the same shift in the way we communicate.) When
speaking of the values inherent in a digital culture, I'm not necessarily referring to a specific age group, although new media
values are most widely held by generation Y (those born between
1980 and 2001).[2] There are always exceptions to the rules, especially when it comes to classifying the characteristics of a large
group of individuals.

Generation Y is unique because of their "generational memory," both remembering the "before" and "after" of the digital
communication revolution. Preceding generations are largely unaware of the influential new media values a digital culture uses
for decision making. As Richard Niebuhr once wrote, "We are in
history as the fish is in water."[3] In other words, just as the ocean
water flows in, over, and through the gills of a fish, the period of
history we live in, or culture, flows in, over, and through us every
waking moment. Moreover, the fish isn't aware of the ocean unless it is forcefully removed from it. If you've ever seen a fish
pulled from the water at the end of a fishing line, you know exactly what I'm talking about.

In the same way, we're largely unaware of the cultural values
that influence our decision making. To put it plainly, our culture is the "ocean" in which we swim. (This is why, for instance,

cross-cultural missions trips are so transformative. We are plucked from our "ocean" and boy, do we feel it! We get a sense of what life is like outside the confines of our comfy, cozy, familiar body of water.) Studies show that the single biggest factor in predicting what values someone will hold is the generation they are born into. Our generational identity influences us more than our socioeconomic status, political affiliation, geographic location, even more than our family of origin. It stands to reason the cultural values of the generation we were born into influence beyond measure—and we're completely unaware of it most of the time.

An illustration: When I first got glasses in the sixth grade, there was a period of time where, instead of the appropriate and beneficial response of looking *through* my glasses, I could not stop looking *at* my glasses. Tragic, I know.

Imagine a gangly kid with a slightly higher-than-normal voice (I was a late bloomer) wandering around the schoolyard in a cross-eyed stupor. Yep, that was me. To use the analogy, the glasses were a foreign object I was unfamiliar with. My glasses quite literally affected my worldview, but it took some getting used to. After what felt like an eternity, my eyes eventually compensated for the lenses that adorned my pimple-ridden face and I could see much better. Go figure. The glasses were the new set of lenses through which I saw the world. Now, I can't imagine not wearing glasses.

In the same way, gen Y has put on new media "glasses," so to speak. It took some time to adjust, but you now have an entire generation seeing more "clearly" than before. Preceding generations (me before glasses) and successive generations (me after glasses) do not "see" what the big fuss is about. This is why the silent and baby boomer generations, as a whole, are dragging their collective feet when it comes to adopting new media values. Why? Simple. It means their vision will be disrupted.

As for generation Z (the terribly creative name for those born between 2002 to present day), their cultural vision has already been adjusted. In a sense, they were born with glasses on. As my friend and fellow college professor asks his students, "Who knows more about computers, you or me?" Inevitably, the students think they do. But my friend Brian, a thirty-five-year-old who remembers the world both before and after new media values, knows more. Way more. He had to learn digital the hard way—by experiencing the transitions as they happened. Now, instead of simply using high-speed Internet, he knows why high-speed is better. His students, largely, do not.

For instance, I remember, with great specificity, first connecting to the Internet as a junior high student via America Online (AOL). My friend (as in one—I didn't have many in junior high; remember, I was a late bloomer!) had it so I needed it too. I convinced my parents to open one of the CDs that AOL shipped to our house on what seemed like a daily basis and take them up on the "10 hours free!" offer.

Ah, AOL. Was there anything better? I fondly remember the delightful screech of a dial-up modem, the painfully slow computer processor speeds, even slower Internet speeds, all crescendoing into the three little words that made everyone's day: "You've got mail!"

Fast-forward to today. I didn't know back then it would've taken me hours to download the latest 2014 chart-topper from iTunes with the Internet speeds we had in 1993. My son, by contrast, will never live in a world where high-speed Internet does not exist. Unlike me, he won't merely *forget* what slow Internet speeds were like. He simply *will not have the capacity* to process a reality where one cannot download an HD movie in the time it takes to pop the popcorn. (For reference, in 1999 my college roommate had a 2 GB hard drive on his computer. We thought it was huge. "How will you ever fill two whole gigabytes?" we thought. "Think of all the Word documents you can hold!" we said. By contrast, in 2014, the typical download size of an HD movie on iTunes is 4 GB. How times have changed!)

Yes, gen Y stands at the crossroads and connects the two—the digital immigrants and digital natives. They serve as the digital bridge, able to recollect life before and after the digital revolution. The glasses took some getting used to, but now their vision is clearer than ever.

Of course, elements of what I'm calling "digital communication" (e.g., email, texting, social media, blogging) have existed in various forms since the 1960s (the first email was sent in 1971 by Ray Tomlinson; the earliest form of what we know as "the Internet"—ARPAnet—went online in 1969, only to crash seconds after its first use!), but it is gen Y who most closely identifies with the values a new media culture has produced. This explains why younger people have embraced digital communication with little to no hesitation. They don't just *do* social; they *are* social.

The aforementioned new media values, interactivity ("Value 1: Looking for a Mouse"), personalization ("Value 2: It's Mine and It's about Me"), ubiquity/connectedness ("Value 3: The Fading Line between Online and Offline"), and sharing ("Value 4: Gather, Distribute, Connect"), each deserve an in-depth dissection. In short, there's gold in them 'thar hills. While these values are not comprehensive, it is my belief they adequately encompass the general *ethos* of a new media culture and, secondarily, describe the driving force behind an entire generation, gen Y.[4]

It's important to study these values objectively. Assigning a value judgment (e.g., "good," "bad," "confusing," "weird") isn't helpful, especially if you find yourself in a generation other than Y. Think of yourself as a social scientist. Imagine you're holding up a gem and your only task is to describe what you're seeing—angles, colors, the way the light refracts, weight, etc. Only, your "gem" is a generation of digital natives. These are the main values digital natives use to assess and make decisions in their everyday lives.

5

VALUE 1: LOOKING FOR A MOUSE

ONE OF MY FAVORITE new media thinkers, author and NYU professor Clay Shirky, tells an anecdotal tale involving a visit to his friend's house. It's as cute as it is telling:

> I was having dinner with a group of friends about a month ago, and one of them was talking about sitting with his four-year-old daughter watching a DVD. In the middle of the movie, she jumps up off the couch and runs around behind the screen. That seems like a cute moment. Maybe she's going back there to see if Dora is really back there or whatever. But that wasn't what she was doing. She started rooting around in the cables. And her dad said, "What are you doing?" She stuck her head out from behind the screen and said, "Looking for the mouse."[1]

"Looking for the mouse." Those words both fascinate and haunt me. Think about the implications of this for a moment. When toddlers consume media, they expect it to be an interactive experience. Two-way instead of one-way. I have a young son, so I can vouch for this phenomenon. After watching him pick up how to use an iPad in less than a day, it shouldn't surprise me when he taps on the television screen in our living room, expecting it to respond to his touch. His world is one where media is responsive and interactive. Period.

This interactive value doesn't just affect toddlers. It affects us all, whether we're aware of it or not. The digital revolution has given us an insatiable thirst for interactivity. We speak, and companies, organizations, and other individuals actually listen. Gone are the days when a few fortunate media conglomerates held the means to broadcast a message to whomever they pleased. Those conglomerates still exist, but the broadcast era has given way to the digital revolution, which favors the little guy. People like you and me. Thanks to social technology, we have the means to say whatever we'd like, to whomever we choose, whenever we want to—for better or worse. In a way, digital communication has given us our voice back.

For instance, in late 2012, Nielsen, the TV ratings authority, introduced a new metric they would be including in their ratings evaluations. The Nielsen Twitter TV Rating "delivers a syndicated-standard metric around the reach of the TV conversation on Twitter."[2] Put simply, this new rating shows how many people are tweeting about the show they're watching. (This is part of the reason you see hashtags in the bottom right-hand corner of many TV shows.) In the U.S., we are becoming a nation of multi-screen media consumers.

When the jerky, self-obsessed dork (thankfully) doesn't get the final rose, when Lady Gaga shows up wearing fresh produce to the Grammys, when yet another celebrity *just* past their prime has a fabled "wardrobe malfunction" during the Super Bowl half-time show (it's almost predictable), we tweet about it. Boy, do we ever. The folks at Nielsen, being "Issachars" for their particular industry, saw the trend and, instead of burying their heads in the sand, decided to do something about it. So they partnered with Twitter to ensure their relevancy for the decades ahead. Smart. Very smart.

Another example comes from Barack Obama's 2008 presidential campaign. It is widely believed he won the election because of his campaign's savvy use of social media. Amongst other things, it gave him the perception of being more accessible—more interactive. For instance, the Obama campaign raised 88 percent of their campaign funding using social networking. Alongside a donations-optimized website and massive email campaign (many of which the candidate wrote himself), the Obama campaign used Facebook, Twitter, and MySpace (yes, *that* MySpace) to haul in a record-setting one-month total of 32 million dollars, 28 million of which was raised online. What's even more fascinating, and pinpoints the power of personability through interactivity, is that 90 percent of those donations were under $100.[3] (2008 also marked the first presidential election where social media made any sort of impact on the results. Think of it as the modern-day version of the televised Nixon vs. Kennedy debate!)

Lastly, my seminary experience is a shining example of the power of interactivity. When I graduated from Bethel Seminary with a Master of Divinity in 2010, I had spent roughly five months physically on campus. Over 80 percent of my degree was earned from my home office and various coffee shops around Des Moines. Many of the courses revolved around online discussion boards, video lectures (both recorded and live), and traditional assignments (e.g., exercises, term papers, thesis statements).

Although there was no public-facing social component (think closed-circuit television), this style of learning enhanced our learning by giving us access to the professors and other students in a way traditional students did not experience. In fact, one of my professors confessed to a group of us distance students, "I actually prefer teaching the distance classes. You're all so much more engaged in class and online!" Of course, I'm a bit biased, but experiencing online learning showed me the power of using interactive technology to connect people to ideas.

Given all the interactivity examples listed above—media, government, education—we would be naïve in assuming the church need not concern itself with innovation. Given the evidence and seeing the impact digital communication is making on the basic building blocks of society, burying our collective heads in the sand would be a poor choice. Yet sadly, this seems to be the emerging trend. When facing the fork in the road, choosing either more or less interactivity, churches seem to be choosing the latter.

THE GREAT TWITTER EXPERIMENT

Take the Twitter experiment conducted by church marketing expert Mickey Mellen. Mickey set out to test the responsiveness—or interactivity level, if you will—of Atlanta-area churches. The test was simple: send a tweet to churches with a Twitter presence asking when their Sunday services were being held. Out of the eleven churches he contacted, sadly only one of them responded.[4] (What makes this worse, in my mind, is that some of the non-responsive churches tweeted something unrelated after Mickey asked his question, effectively ignoring his request.)

While serving as the executive director for the Center for Church Communication, we found this to be a pervasive trend as well. Churches we spoke to cited limited staff resources, lack of volunteer help, and lack of interest or demand amongst the congregation as reasons that kept them from providing more online content and services. In fact, one popular Lifeway study showed 40 percent of respondent churches having no active social presence at all.[5]

As researcher and author, Brian Solis is fond of saying, "Engage or die." This statement, although stark, is *just* this side of hyperbole. Let me be clear: the church and her mission will *never* perish. This much we know. What we *do not* know is what our co-creative role in building God's kingdom will be. We do not know because it is mostly up to us. We can choose to become interactive as a church or we can choose to fade further into the cultural background.

SERVING AN INTERACTIVE GOD

But fear not! There is a way forward. We may start out this section by asking, "What does an interactive church look like?" How does a church with new media values "do ministry" (for lack of a better term) in the twenty-first century?

For starters, we must acknowledge the fact that we serve an interactive God. The God of the Holy Bible is one very different than the deities history has repeatedly produced. We need look no further than the life of Jesus—Immanuel, or "God with us"—to see *Yahweh* is one who enjoys getting his hands dirty.

Many pagan cultures have stories similar to the ones found in the pages of the Bible. Mesopotamian cultures had very similar stories, some even predating the Old Testament versions. Even the cornerstone of Christianity itself, the death and resurrection of Jesus Christ, has reflections in pagan mythology (particularly the story of Marduk).

But what all of these stories are missing is the "earthiness" of God the Father. In fact, when considering the entirety of

Scripture and the characteristics of God, one would not be surprised to learn God methodically chose stories like Noah and the flood to make an even sharper point. The message? The God of the Bible wants the message to resound loud and clear: "I am that I am." In other words, God is unlike any deity you've ever dreamed of. He is completely, totally, categorically beyond categorization. He is, in a word, *other*.

To put this into play, when we see an early Mesopotamian cultural version of the flood, the gods act as petulant, defiant, impish toddlers, spiteful because they did not get their way. They seem quite pleased to endlessly torture the Noah character of the play. You must understand, narrative pieces like this actively reflect the cultural perspective of who people of this era understood God (or gods) to be. In this culture, folks believed if they acted properly, said and did the right things, and didn't "step out of line," then maybe, *just maybe*, the gods would leave them alone long enough to squeeze some small amount of joy out of life. Even then, the gods were mischievous enough to inflict great amounts of pain on you, simply because they could.

Sounds miserable, doesn't it? And yet, so many of us live our lives with the same understanding of the God of the Bible. "He'll leave me alone as long as I don't step out of line." As goes our theology (or, "one's thoughts about God"), so goes our behavior.

I believe this predicament is precisely why Scripture includes the story of Noah and the flood. What do we see through the eyes of the author of Genesis? We see a tender, compassionate, thoughtful being whose vision for humanity compels him to create another way forward. While the pagan gods take great joy in the demise of humanity, *Yahweh* mourns what has become of his beloved jewel of creation, yet declares solemnly, "This isn't the end of the story."

The writer of the flood narrative, under direction of the Holy Spirit, compels readers to believe there is a God who cherishes each and every human soul. By contrasting the Hebrew account against story lines from other cultures, God rebukes the pervasive, long-standing, faulty theology of the day while revealing his true nature that declares, "I am actively involved in your life. I am approachable. I am for you. I am here." God, in a word, is interactive. (Selah. Pause, and calmly think on that.)

Further, God's word to us—the Holy Scriptures—provides an experience unlike any other written piece of history. It is, by nature, *interactive*, "alive and powerful" as described by the writer of Hebrews.[6]

When I was young in my relationship with Jesus, I remember declaring to a mentor, "The Bible is like a 'choose-your-own-adventure' book!" The statement, while painfully naïve, reflects the true nature of the Bible: engaging the active mind and heart of a living God through the pages of a printed book. Reading the Bible is unlike reading other books in that its primary purpose is not *transactional* (i.e., reading to gain a benefit embedded in the text itself; improve your golf swing, write better, learn Spanish, etc.), but *relational*. Simply put, we read Scripture with the promise that we will come to know or acquire a more intimate understanding of who God is and how he operates in our world.

SPIRITUAL INTERACTIVITY IN THE DIGITAL AGE

Seeing how God is interactive, and seeing how we have been created in his image, it stands to reason we are, by nature, interactive. Church history shows us—from the earliest disciples on the shores of Galilee to the Augustinian monks to which Luther belonged to the underground Christian movement in China—

followers of Jesus have always gathered together. These collective gatherings have many facets, but one of the main purposes is, at root, interactive in nature. We gather to interact with other members of the body and the Spirit that animates us.

These interactive gatherings have taken many forms over the years: "agape feasts" of the early Christian community, which included a shared meal together, complete with wine, meat, salt, and milk; the Herrnhut model of the Moravians; the acapella worship services of the Church of Christ; Bonhoeffer gathering his small group of disciples at Finkenwalde; the Billy Graham revival meetings.

But what do gatherings look like for the twenty-first century church? As technology emerges in our congregations, how does a digitally responsive church incorporate a vast, growing, and diverse online population into the "flock"? Where does a local congregation's responsibility "end," so to speak, when caring for the spiritual needs of people who, for a myriad of reasons, may never step foot inside of a physical church building? When does a church have a responsibility to intentionally build an online ministry just as they would an adult ministry or Sunday school program?

One solution can be found at Omaha-based Christ Community Church and their online pastor, Robert Murphy. Robert leads the Christ Community online campus by serving as the "shepherd" for the cyber community. The church streams two weekly services live through the online campus, located at www. CCCOmaha.tv. Additionally, a chat room is moderated every week during the service, allowing participants to interact with Robert, his online team, and other visitors. For the folks who visit the online campus site, church isn't something you passively sit and watch. Church becomes something you actively participate in—

asking questions, encouraging others from around the world, and responding to God's Word—all online. This approach is not without its foibles (we'll get into that later), but it's a good first step. And, as the saying goes, the goal is "progress, not perfection."

RUBBING ELBOWS

An interactive church goes into the nooks and crannies of the web, fearlessly living out their online lives with purpose and vigor. It's a concept I call "rubbing elbows." When we look at the life of Jesus, we see a man who, being God, could have rightfully chosen to circle up in a holy huddle. He fully embraced all the qualities of being human, yet he never tripped up once. *Not even once.* (To put this into context, in the time it took me to write the previous paragraph, I got super jealous of a Facebook friend's hand-crank coffee grinder. Coveting much? FAIL.)

Jesus charged headlong into a culture far away from perfect. The world Jesus lived in was rife with paganism, idolatry, infidelity, cheats, swindlers, fakes, phonies, cowards, and hypocrites. Yet his position was not to head *away* from the human-centric drama and chaos. His instinct was to valiantly stride into the cesspool of the human experience and get dirty. In short, he rubbed elbows with the saint and sinner alike—entering our world rather than planning his exit from it. Jesus as a man was highly interactive with nearly everyone around him. (I say "nearly" because, much like present-day, it is those who believe they are closest to God who are, in fact, the furthest. The religious elite did not like Jesus and chose to distance themselves from him.)

I believe our online lives can and should reflect these exact principles. With digital communication tools like online campuses and social networks, we as followers of Jesus quite literally possess the ability to "go into all the world," bringing the light and life of God with us. Practically speaking, we can use online connection points to facilitate relational connections with those we may never get the chance to interact with normally.

For instance, I have a friend named Kristina. Kristina is a self-proclaimed atheist and the host of a video podcast based in the Twin Cities. Amongst other subjects, Kristina frequently delves into the topic of faith. Every so often, I will appear on her show, brought in under the assumption I would be arguing the "pro-God" position, with Kristina serving as antagonist.

We've only had a couple of thirty-minute on-air conversations, but the dialogue continues long after I leave the studio through various avenues like Twitter, Facebook, text, and email. One could make the argument that relationships have always been maintained outside of common interest points (e.g., a video podcast). While this is true, digital communication provides easy points of relational transmission between two or more parties. In other words, she can see what I'm up to on a daily basis, even when I'm not physically present. Whereas before the digital revolution I would have had to pick up the phone and call Kristina or write a letter, now I can refresh my Twitter feed and see what's going on *right now*. Increased relational contact points increase the frequency of connection, which increases the potential for intimacy. (Intimacy, for those wondering, holds its own definition: "Into-me-see." Trite? Perhaps. Effective? Definitely. Intimacy means intentionally giving someone a peek behind the masks in your life.)

The benefit of rubbing elbows online is clear. Kristina, as an atheist, gets to see how a normal, everyday Christian like me lives his life online—for better or for worse. When I tweet about going on a date with my wife, share a quote from the latest book

I'm reading, or live-tweet the latest episode of *The Bachelor* (don't judge), Kristina sees a person who is, for the most part, very similar. With a few notable exceptions (like, oh, I don't know, the whole believing "Jesus is the Son of God" thing), our lives are remarkably similar. As one of my son's favorite books says, "Joys are the same, and love is the same. Pain is the same, and blood is the same . . . wherever we are, all over the world."[7] There is something powerful about the phrase "Me too!"

Digital communication did not suddenly, magically make me or Kristina into different people. These tools simply helped bridge the relational gap between the times we get to personally interact. As author and church planter Alan Hirsch once said during a conference I attended, "the Gospel is transmitted along relational lines."

The more we rub elbows online with normal, everyday people who may not know Jesus, the more we break down the barriers between "us" (Christians) and "them" (non-Christians). Being a true representative of yourself online allows those "relational lines" to remain constant and available 24/7. Also, judgment of a people group isn't as easy when the "them" has a face attached to it.

WHAT'S LOVE GOT TO DO WITH IT?

Here's an important reminder: rubbing elbows with people online does not mean proselytizing with every status update. Why? Because it's (usually) not an authentic representation of who you are as an individual. Most of us have interests, hobbies, careers—indeed, *lives*—outside the four walls of a church. Rubbing elbows online means we "tear the veil" that shrouds our lives with the hopes of showing what a Christian's life looks like, warts and all.

Whatever your "extracurriculars" are, find a way to pull them into your online life as well. Don't neglect who you are as a person because you feel undue pressure to only talk about your faith.

Imagine you're passing through the greatest city on the planet, Des Moines, and we sit down for coffee. Now imagine the only thing I talk about between latte sips is my wife, Kerry. At first you might think, "Oh, that's cute. That guy really loves his wife!" (It's true, I do.) But after a while, if the only thing I talk about is what my wife eats, what she was wearing when she left the house, all the dates we've had, etc., it would probably get irritating. No, actually, I'm *sure* it would get irritating. In fact, you'd probably start to think something was wrong with me. Needy, codependent, and "crippled with insecurity" are all terms that come to mind. Our conversation would most likely leave you feeling awkward, uncomfortable, and completely ignored as a person. And you'd have good reason to feel this way. I learned nothing about you. All I did was obsessively talk about my wife.

Take this relational dynamic and put it into an online context. What if the only thing I talked about online was my wife? How weird would that be? For instance, we've all seen the guy, usually a youth pastor (no offense to my youth worker brethren), who tweets constantly about how "hottttt" his wife is. Or the person who puts nothing but "date night" pictures with her boyfriend on her Instagram feed. Or the guy who won't stop referring to his wife as his "bride." Ugh.

On some level, these relational idiosyncrasies are to be commended. Nothing brings me greater joy than seeing people appropriately live out their love online for the cherished ones in their lives. But people who constantly refer back to an important relationship—online or off—are either: (1) codependent, (2) jealous, (3) fearful, or (4) a toxic mix of the three. These are the people I find myself disengaging from most often. My guess is you do too.

If I talk about other things online beside my marriage, does it mean I no longer love my wife? Heavens, no! Our marriage has a profound influence on how I live my day-to-day life. But what I share online includes a lot more than being married, even though I'm very much in love with my wife.

The correlation here should be clear. As Christians, we are very much in love with the person of Jesus. Our relationship with him forms the cornerstone for which we base all of our thoughts, wishes, hopes, dreams—our very *lives*. But there comes a point where you must start living *from* your identity in Christ rather than talking *about* your identity in Christ.

Unfortunately, I see too many Christians online who believe they are being faithful when, to the rest of the world, they come off as obnoxious. If someone's social stream is filled with nothing but Bible verses, references to "the blood of the Lamb," and yet another Foursquare check-in at their church, I ask myself, "Why? What's the motivation behind this?" Since motives are notoriously hard to judge (read: impossible), this is emotional thin ice to tread on. I think author Donald Miller summed up this struggle well on his blog:

> The reality is, Jesus doesn't need for us to put on a show. He doesn't need for us to kneel in the end zone, engage in controlling conversations or argue theology over twitter. Instead, there is power in quiet, private spirituality. If we want to see change, we can pray, and we can have one-on-one conversations. When we switch from a loud, showy public faith to a private, quiet faith we will find God begins to work and we don't have to work as hard.[8]

Again, judging one's motives is rarely productive. Only God has the ability to do this purely. But one must tend to their own heart and ask what motivates their decisions—both offline and on. As Jesus warns us in the gospel of Matthew, "Be especially careful when you are trying to do good so that you don't make a performance out of it."[9] Live your life so people would not be surprised to learn you follow Jesus. Live your life imagining you can only tell people you're a Christian with your deeds, not your words.

SMOKE SIGNALS AND THEOLOGY

In *Amusing Ourselves to Death*, Neil Postman plainly states, "You cannot use smoke to do philosophy."[10] He's referring to smoke signals the Cherokee once used to communicate messages to far-off tribal members. These signals were effectively used to communicate the basics: *Help! Food! We're over here! Stay away!* Smoke signals, however, would be ineffective at communicating the complexities of, say, Descartes' epistemological statement of *cogito ergo sum*. The communicative agent in question, smoke signals, do not inherently possess the ability to communicate complex meaning. "Its form excludes the content." To put it in modern-day terms, smoke signals have a character limit.

In the spirit of this statement, I would argue one cannot "do" evangelism with smoke signals. Yet, this is the method so many of us rely on. We do the life-giving message of Jesus a disservice with misleading questions like, "If you were to die tonight, do you know where you would end up?"

The question, while well-intentioned, is like trying to use a smoke signal to convey the gospel message. It doesn't work. The method is wrong. When you misuse a communicative medium,

frustration inevitably ensues. You can't read a DVD player man-
ual the same way you read a love letter. One does not equal the
other. Similarly, you cannot do evangelism, the true hard work
of rubbing elbows with someone who doesn't know Jesus, over
social media. It just doesn't work.

The "outside world" often views Christians and our attempts
to evangelize the way we view aggressive salesmen on infomercials. We come across as having something to sell—aggressively
heaping on benefits and ramping up the rhetoric, wearing down
potential buyers until they finally acquiesce to our "But wait!
There's more!" demands.

The motivation for these things (slamming our social networks with religious content) is good and pure. We want people to
know the God who has changed our lives. This is to be celebrated
and affirmed. It is a natural reaction to being in love.

But this is where the two-way nature of social media can
teach us something about building God's kingdom. I am at
my worst when I'm forcefully pushing information into people's online information streams. Endlessly promoting a blog
post, my latest offering, or an ebook gets on people's nerves.
It sounds corny, but people don't care how much you know (or
what you have to share, sell, or suggest) until they know how
much you care.

Same holds true for the nature of evangelism. When we look
at the life of Jesus, we see a man who clearly had a message to
share. Yet we also see a man who took the time to enter the lives
of the people he met. Listening to the Samaritan woman at the
well tell her sordid story of relational messiness, Jesus was quite
content to enter her world. There was give (John 4:17b NIV: "You
have no husband," ZING!) and there was take (John 4:7 NIV:
"Will you give me a drink?"), but most importantly, there was *re-*

lationship. There was a genuine interest in who this woman was, where she had been, and what would bring her the most exciting life moving forward.

Jesus was also not afraid to divulge details of his own life or to engage in intimacy with this Samaritan woman. For instance, the very act of speaking to a Samaritan was, shall we say, dicey. Add to the fact she was, well, a *she*, you've got the makings of a bona fide scandal.

In Jesus' day, women of any culture weren't particularly valued, much less a woman who had been divorced and remarried multiple times. The fact she was going to the well by herself, in the middle of the day, shows she was deeply ashamed and/or outcast by her own people.

Think about it. When do you use the most water during the day? Give yourself a pat on the back if you said morning. This poor woman waited it out until midday to avoid the sarcastic barbs and steely cold looks from her community.

Adding to the complexity, we can clearly see the discomfort the disciples have when they arrive on the scene. John tells us they were "shocked" to see him talking to a woman. In this era, women did not speak to men who were not either their father or husband.

To happen upon Jesus speaking to a random woman would truly be jarring for the disciples. It would be like coming home and finding your dad sitting on the front step, chatting with a known prostitute. Your reaction would parallel that of the disciples. John tells us that none of them had the nerve to say, "Um, Jesus, just what is it you're trying to accomplish here? Why are you talking to *her*? What are people going to think?" Jesus is more rebellious than Sunday school flannel boards have led us to believe.

This is the setting for a profound act of self-disclosure by Jesus: he reveals to the woman who he *truly* is. Many times throughout the gospels, Jesus purposefully shrouds his messianic identity. But in John 4:26, Jesus tells the woman at the well plainly, "I am the Messiah!"[11] In the gospel of John, this is the first time he's ever spoken about himself in such a way. He doesn't share first with his people or his disciples, but a lowly Samaritan—and a woman, no less! St. John is making a big-time point here. He's saying, "Pay attention to this. It's really important." The technical term is the "Law of First Mention," but basically it's a Scripture writer's way of bolding, underlining, and italicizing something, all at the same time.

John's gospel is written with the purpose of showing Jesus as the Messiah, so the "first mention" of his true identity can't be overlooked. By telling the Samaritan woman who he is, he's declaring, "God desires relationship with *all* people, not just the Israelites."

Make no mistake about it, John's intention is highly strategic. Original readers of the text would have been floored by the inherent meaning of this passage. By this one, calculated act of defiance, Jesus is smashing all the pedigrees people claimed that would make themselves acceptable to God. In this moment, Jesus says by his actions, "It doesn't matter if you're an Israelite or Samaritan, it doesn't matter where you've been or what you've done; it doesn't matter if you're 'religious' or not, a relationship with God is freely and openly available to you. Come, follow me!" That, my friends, is good news.

Again, Christians can learn from this model how to behave online. A good rule of thumb to use is the 80/20 law: 80 percent of the time, your social content should solely add value to your online community. No "asks," no event invites, no promotional tweets, no invitations to church services, no bake sale invites, no pleading for volunteers—nothing of the sort for 80 percent of your social media content.

At this point you might be thinking two things: (1) "Then what in the world am I *supposed* to share?" (2) "But Justin, tweeting about the four horsemen of the Apocalypse is the most valuable thing I can share with my community! They need to see their sin and turn to God for repentance!" My answers: (1) We'll get to that in a minute. (2) At the risk of setting up a straw man (the example above is obvious hyperbole), I'd say we're now living in an opt-in economy. If people don't like what you're saying, they will simply tune you out. It's that simple. (And last time I checked, most non-Christians have a very low tolerance for Revelation. Come to think of it, so do most Christians!)

To round out your social content allocation, 20 percent of the time you can make "asks." That may even be a bit high. *New York Times* bestselling author Gary Vaynerchuck poignantly explained this paradigm in an interview when he said, "Listen, faith institutions don't get traction with their social media presence because no one in their community believes they care."[12] When you simply blast people with information and don't invite them into a true, mutual conversation, it's painfully obvious.

BARTH AND DIGITAL NATIVES

Martin Luther is credited as saying, "If you preach the gospel in all aspects with the exception of the issues which deal specifically with your time—you are not preaching the gospel at all."[13] The issues in this chapter are those of our "time." The church can no longer pretend social media does not apply to its local expressions. We must intelligently ask ourselves the question, just as

Luther did. "How can we use technology to build God's kingdom here on earth?" For him, it was the printing press. For us, it's a social technology—using it in a way that facilitates relationship-building opportunities like never before. Again it is worth stating, "the Gospel is transmitted along relational lines."

Karl Barth once stated we should do theology with the Bible in one hand and the daily newspaper in the other. I believe he means we need to be appropriately connected to the surrounding culture we find ourselves in. We need to know as much about what's happening on Main Street as we do in Malachi. If we can impeccably parse Greek verbs but can't name our neighbors, we have failed as Christians. There is a certain "cultural pulse" we must be familiar with as followers of Jesus. The pulse of our time, friends, is driven by the strong, steady rhythms of social.

THE CRESTING WAVE OF LEADERSHIP TRANSITION

We're also facing a transition in the leadership of local congregations. Baby boomers are beginning to retire and hand over the baton of leadership to emerging generations. Younger leaders are being asked to step into leadership roles they may feel woefully unprepared for. It's the perfect storm of leadership challenges. Not only is the culture changing, but the visionary landscape of the local church is shifting as well.

Practically speaking, what does this mean?

For starters, young leaders have an opportunity to write their own destiny. They can humbly ask established generations to teach them the timeless principles of effective ministry—timeless principles that transcend culture and trends—or trudge blindly forward to their own detriment. Asking questions like, "What has worked in building church community?" "How do I increase tithes and offerings?" "What does it take to become more effective at sharing the essence of the gospel message?" and, "What is the foundation of a spirited, growing, and Christ-centered church and how can new media values be applied to these areas?" These are questions young leaders need to be asking.

Established leaders in the twilight of their ministry career, on the other hand, will be remembered by how they navigate this transition. Did you set the next generation up for success, extending the leadership baton and allowing new leaders to pave their own way forward? Or did you bury your head in the sand, content to wait out your days in blissful ignorance, hoping the new media wave doesn't crest before you retire? Did you shrink back from the changing cultural landscape, or did you lean into the tension? As an older leader, you may not understand the digital culture. But your legacy is dependent upon how well you navigate the transition and set up the emerging generation for success. Interactivity isn't just something a new media culture demands. It's something younger leaders need from those who have gone before them.

6

VALUE 2: IT'S MINE AND IT'S ABOUT ME

I WAS LOOKING THROUGH my old CD case recently, struck with the thought of how quaint they seemed. Page after page of CDs, each disc having memory after memory tied to it. High school dances, college frat parties, driving alone at night, memorable nights spent with my wife—all tied up in circular pieces of plastic.

Do you remember the first CD you ever bought? I do. It was 1994 and I saved up my allowance to buy *Jock Rock Volume 1*. The *Jock Rock* series were curated albums of arena anthems you'd hear at pro sports games—NBA, NFL, MLB, etc. Some of the gems from *Volume 1* included "Tequila" by the Champs and "Blitzkrieg Bop" by the Ramones. (I think I bought this CD specifically to make myself feel like a world-class athlete, even though I was literally the worst player on every team I had ever been on. I had the legs of a newborn gazelle, couldn't hit the broadside of a barn, and had to wear pads on my forearms in junior high football because I bruised so badly. Tragic.) If you want a review, *Jock Rock* was good, but it wasn't great. It was basically a hybrid classic rock/oldies station with Chris Berman soundbites ran-domly scattered throughout the album. (I'm convinced his album cameos are why I don't like "Boomer" to this day.) There were a few songs I liked, but most were completely skippable.

If you're a student of media evolution like I am, one of the crowning glories of the compact disc was the ability to *skip* tracks with the click of a button. Gone were the days where you had to fast-forward through a cassette tape, hoping you could somehow sense the gap between the song the producers threw on the album to get it out the door and your favorite tune. Now you could track ahead and pass over the junky songs and get to your favorite one with ease. The compact disc was truly a giant leap forward for media ecology.

It's 2014 and I could not tell you the last CD I purchased. With the advent of iTunes, introduced in 2001 by then Apple CEO Steve Jobs, the entire music industry changed seemingly overnight. CDs instantly became outdated technology. The era of personalized music—the very personalization of a culture—was ushered in with the click of a mouse. iTunes had been bubbling behind the scenes for years, but the winds of change coalesced in 2001 to make the decades-long vision a reality. But it also marked the beginning of a new era in our culture: the ability to customize nearly everything.

Take my beloved *Jock Rock* for instance. If I had to consider purchasing this album on iTunes today, only two songs would make the cut (the tracks from James Brown and Sly & The Family Stone, in case you were wondering). Everything else? Thanks, but no thanks. But just fifteen short years ago, buying only these two songs was not a possibility.

This type of hyper-personalized control is changing more than the way we listen to music. iTunes is a metaphor for the shifting twenty-first century landscape. We are no longer required to accept things we do not like, want, or need. We have the ability to customize our world to suit our needs as we see fit. Don't want to watch commercials? Skip through them. Don't like your uncle's political Facebook rants? Hide him (and he'll never even know!). Want to know what's going on in your hometown, even if you're thousands of miles away? Check out the local newspaper's website and catch up on all the action. With digital communication, personalization—or, arranging things as you desire them to be—is king. Geography, relational ties, and artistic intentions are all, it seems, relative.

Before the iTunes era, you had to endure songs you didn't particularly enjoy, wait for your favorite television show to air in its scheduled time slot, and listen to full sermons when the pastor should have landed the plane ten minutes into the message.

While this new worldview certainly has its benefits, it can exacerbate the problem of an already "me-centered" species. One need not read very far in Scripture to see the effects of self-centeredness. Luther described it as *incurvatus in se*, or "life turned inward" on itself rather than outward toward God and others. We need no lessons in selfishness, this much is true.

HOW PERSONALIZATION APPLIES TO THE CHURCH

Translation preferences, online campuses, programs and events, podcasts, and even church attendance are subject to personalization. We can decide how and when we go to church, what translation we most prefer, and what preacher or pastor we most resonate with. (Remember, the goal isn't to cast judgment. Our job is to simply observe, take note, and make decisions accordingly.)

Some may say the value of personalization will usher in an era where Christians simply omit the truths of Christianity they find unfavorable and oblige those they find palatable. News flash: Christians have *always* been doing this. Whether it was the Gnostic heresies, the Pelagian heresy of the early church, or Thomas Jefferson literally chopping out portions of Scripture he found to be "nonsense" (namely the miracles of Jesus), Christians have always fell victim to a cut-and-paste theology. In short, social media isn't creating the problem; it's merely giving a persistent theological thorn another side to rest in.

If we allow it, I believe the iTunes era will present one of the greatest opportunities the church has ever seen. As the church becomes increasingly networked, as we become a truly global entity, we will finally begin to see how the Spirit of Jesus works through all facets of the church, not just our immediate, mostly local context. For instance, Christians in North America will see how vastly different the expression of the gospel is for believers in South America. American Christianity tends to focus on becoming, acquiring, and achieving, while the South American gospel centers on freedom from oppression, justice, and all the wrongs in the world finally being made right. Same gospel. Same Jesus. Two sides of the same coin.

Personalization will allow us to more fully express the work of God in our lives, while simultaneously being exposed to the work of God in others. Through digital communication, we can see how God is moving on the other side of the planet while remaining connected to a local church context.

7

VALUE 3: THE FADING LINE BETWEEN ONLINE AND OFFLINE

AS I WRITE THIS, I am 30,000 feet above your head. Quite possibly directly above yours if you live somewhere in between Nashville and Des Moines. Yet, I'm still sending and receiving emails, answering tweets from folks at the conference I just attended, and getting advice from my Facebook friends on how to win the epic armrest battle I'm having with the woman next to me. ("Start scratching your arm, mumbling something about a rash." I did. I won. Hooray fake rashes!)

Why do I share this with you? For starters, it's amazing. WiFi access has been available on airplanes for years, but it still mesmerizes me every time I connect up in the air. Most mornings I struggle with using our juicer correctly, so the fact that someone figured out how to beam a WiFi signal into space, bounce it off a satellite, and into my computer on an airplane moving 500 mph baffles me.

More importantly, this example shows the depths of how dependent we have become on technology. Before you read any further, I need to clarify something. It's tempting to say something like, "It is a severe oversimplification to say technology ubiquitousness is 'bad' or 'good.'" The question we need to answer is, "What are the unintended consequences of social technology?"

I'm wearing a Nike FuelBand on my left wrist right now. It's a device you wear like a watch, but it measures various biorhythms such as your daily step count, calories burned, and how you're doing with your daily activity goals. As you accomplish different milestones, you can share them with your social networks. My wife and I even have a fun little competition going with who can rack up the most fuel points. (We're synced up on the iPhone app and can see each other's progress throughout the day.)

The FuelBand is interesting because it embeds technology onto my body, tracking my movements and automatically sharing them with those in my social circles. It's something I wear 24/7. It is always with me. It's technology that is, quite literally, ubiquitous. The power of the FuelBand lies in its ability to leverage my online tribe for the sake of making me more active. Another app on my phone encourages Facebook friends to cheer me on as I take my daily jog. When someone likes my status update, the app briefly quiets the music in my headphones and floods my ears with a round of applause. The line between "offline" and "online" is once again blurred.

Devices like the FuelBand are just the beginning. Google revealed "Glass," a cyborg-like set of eyeglasses that displays real-time information to the wearer on the inside of one of the lenses. Think *Terminator* but with less Arnold. I imagine one of the more helpful uses of Google Glass will be when we forget someone's name. Eventually, devices like this will be able to recognize who it is we're speaking to and, through the vast amount of search data available on the web, display their name indiscreetly on the inside of our eyeglasses.

Apple and other tech giants are excitedly drawing up plans for smart watches, essentially computers we wear on our wrist. These devices will be able to beam information back and forth to our smartphones, presumably for the purpose of conveying this information to our social circles. Wearable technology will give way to nanotechnology, permanently blurring the lines between physical and digital.

Technology is becoming embedded into nearly every facet of society. Our refrigerators can tell us when we're running low on certain items. Our cars speak to us, able to reroute us instantaneously depending on traffic patterns or if we've missed our exit. Our mobile phones can automatically tell loved ones when we're approaching an agreed upon meeting spot. As Tina Fey wrote in her painfully humorous autobiography, *Bossypants*, "Technology doesn't move backwards. No society de-industrializes."[1] It's a brave new world, and we get to help shape it.

THE BIRTH OF REAL-TIME MEDIA

Remember the 2013 Super Bowl? The Baltimore Ravens faced off against the San Francisco 49ers in one of the most memorable Super Bowls to date. Why? For starters, the two head coaches, Jim Harbaugh and John Harbaugh, were brothers. This was the first time in any major sporting event, football or otherwise, such a thing had occurred. (Imagine being their parents!)

Second, the lights in the New Orleans Super Dome went out for about thirty minutes in the second half. One entire side of the stadium went dark due to a failure in the power grid rigged specifically for the game. Oops.

While the Ravens ended up winning the game, there was another winner that night. It wasn't a team, player, coach, or bigwig sitting in a box seat. It was a brand. More specifically, Oreo. (To be even more precise, it was the ad agency behind Oreo, 360i. More on them in a bit.) "Team Oreo," perhaps unbeknownst to them at the time, ushered in a new era of ubiquitous, real-time media advertising with a gem that may not look like much (an oreo in a dark space with the text, "You can still dunk in the dark"), but marked a completely different way brands must think through advertising in the social media space. Why? Because this ad went from conception to creation to approval to delivery in less than fifteen minutes. For those unfamiliar with the advertising world, this is an *astounding accomplishment*. To translate this into church terms, think of it as brainstorming, planning, and executing an Easter service in thirty minutes or less. Now do you see what I mean?

The agency I mentioned above who was responsible for producing the ad, 360i, had all hands on deck the night of the Super Bowl. Agency president Sarah Hofstetter explains, "It was easy to get approvals [from the Oreo execs] and get it up in minutes." But a situation like this isn't for the faint of heart. Hofstetter warned, "You need a brave brand to approve content that quickly. When all of the stakeholders come together so quickly, you've got magic." In my favorite part of the interview, Hofstetter explained, "What happens when everything changes, when you go off script? That was where it got fun."[2]

When technology is used properly; when the limits of creativity, of "what is possible?" are pushed; when smart, forward-thinking people put their heads together and think of new ways to do old things, *that's* when things get fun. I don't need to tell you this has implications for the church. If you're reading this book, you already know this.

REAL-TIME CONNECTION

According to Google, desktops will be irrelevant by the time you read this. Access to social networks is now being done primarily through a mobile device. Villages in Africa don't have access to clean drinking water, yet the people huddle around car batteries to charge their mobile devices for two hours per day. This is insane. This is our world. This may make you uncomfortable, which is completely understandable. But the goal is to better understand the culture in which we find ourselves, not to pass value judgments on the values themselves.

Again, in the words of Cynthia Ware:

> Rising from the convergence of new communication and information technologies, these new facilities include instantaneous communication (including one-to-one, one-to-many, many-to-one, and many-to-many), interactivity, peer-to-peer sharing options, extended social networking, and the nurturing of virtual communities. Through wikis, e-books, innovation jams, podcasts, vodcasts, blogs, and etc., collective interactivity and participatory communications abound and are transforming our ability to connect, collaborate, and converse on a global scale in real-time.[3]

The connectedness value emerges from requiring real-time access from everywhere and anywhere to anywhere. This "access" is 24/7, on-demand, and pervasive, regardless of geography.

The emerging "always on" generation connectedness requires a new skill of determining when and how one connects. Limitations previously in place—Internet speed, WiFi coverage, mobile device functionality—are no longer in place. In fact, estimates are by the year 2015, the entire world will be wired in some form or fashion, either through satellite or tower coverage. In short, the excuse of, "I couldn't get any cell coverage!" won't hold water much longer.

In early 2013, a new pope, Francis I, was chosen after an aging Pope Benedict retired early. In a widely circulated picture, we can see clearly how quickly the connectedness value has emerged (see link in the Notes section).[4]

In a side-by-side comparison, we see the ordination of Pope Benedict in 2005 on top. On the bottom, we see the ordination of Pope Francis. The contrast is so stark, it's almost comical. In 2005, the group featured is attentively watching the installation activities. Eyes straight forward, focused on the action.

The 2013 group, however, paints a much different picture. Virtually every person in the photograph is illuminated by the glow of a mobile device. Each device is pointing toward the action, capturing the activity for the world to see. An individual in the 2013 side might be using their mobile for a number of different reasons: taking pictures or video for archival purposes ("I want to show this to my kids someday!"), recording for news or informational purposes ("I need a clip of this for my blog!"), or to share with their social networks ("I'm going to tweet this!").

Regardless of the reason, every person in the photo values connectedness as evidenced by the mobile device adoption that facilitates the connection. We value connectedness because we value sharing. To be connected is to let others into our world for however brief the moment might be.

IN HEAVEN THERE IS NO BEER . . .

I went to an Iowa Hawkeyes game not too long ago, and it was fascinating to see the attire of everyone. As I looked around

Kinnick Stadium, each section alternated Hawkeye colors: black, gold, black, gold. At first, I thought it was random. But the sheer volume of people wearing the same colors in the same sections hinted at a coordinated effort.

I started to wonder, "How did they do this? And why didn't I get the memo?!" So I did a little research. I went to their Facebook page and found specific instructions for what colors to wear in each section. The announcement simply said: All EVEN sections wear gold, all ODD sections wear black.

That was it. If you were to look at this scene from an aerial view, you can see the carefully formed stripes of black and gold formed around the stadium. All of this was coordinated using social media. This is the power of new media to move people.

In Iran and Egypt social media has been used to organize mass demonstrations and protests to combat oppressive governments.

This is how real movements are started.

This is how people network with real-world results.

I think it's important we understand our responsibility to use this power of new media to our advantage to spread the gospel.

Flash mobs gather in an "informed spontaneity" all over the world, imploring people to freeze like mannequins in Grand Central Station, help a would-be groom pop the question to his unassuming, soon-to-be blushing bride, and even throw a giant dance party for Oprah!

Increasingly, relational connections are starting to form primarily online. The social web is turning into a relationship catalyst, spurring people to create, act, change, and meet in new and interesting ways. It is normal now for us to connect with people online before we meet them in person. (In fact, I would say this order is actually becoming *more* normal. It's the new *norming norm*, so to speak.) Connectedness facilitates relationship. Our phones and mobile devices can serve as a portal that tells us about the world around us. Applications like Yelp and AroundMe make it possible for us to use our devices to interpret our reality.

Technology is all around us, and the pace is quickening. Will the church keep pace?

8

VALUE 4: LIFE AMPLIFICATION

THOMAS L. FRIEDMAN INTRODUCES a concept in his book *The World Is Flat* that has staggering implications for the church. He calls it "informing" and defines it as: "Becoming your own self-directed and self-empowered researcher, editor, and selector of entertainment without having to go to the library or the movie theater or through network television."[1] In other words, through everyday search engines like Google, Bing, and Yahoo!, we have limitless information and knowledge at our fingertips. The web has given us all we need to track down the information of our choosing.

I would go one step further in his definition and tack on "... or to church." Social technology has changed the role of the church in society from possessor and dispenser of religious/spiritual knowledge as a commodity to communal hub that sends and receives members, empowering them for the work of ministry.

It used to be that one would have to go to a local church on Sunday morning to receive religious instruction from an individual, usually a white, middle-aged male in the role of pastor, priest, or reverend. The stated nonverbal message in these environments is classic supply and demand. The pastor is supplying something the congregation needs (religious instruction in a communal setting). It is entirely a one-way street. Pastor speaks, congregation listens. The environment reflects this relationship. The pews or rows of seats all face the same direction, usually toward the front, with the focal point being a stage of some sort. These environments aren't only unsuitable for sharing, they actually discourage it. Church buildings, by design, are not built for engagement.

While this format certainly continues to dominate most North American churches, social technology has given us a peek into the life of churches across the world. For instance, if you go to iTunes, click on the podcasts tab, and navigate to the Christianity section, you will find thousands upon thousands of churches with more messages and sermons than one could ever hope to listen to in an entire lifetime. What this means is we can now have our demand met (religious instruction) *outside* the walls of our local church. Practically speaking, we don't need to go to church to hear a message or sermon. As the presiding bishop of the Evangelical Lutheran Church in America, Mark Hanson, puts it, "No longer is the role of the church to own and distribute information. The role of the church is to gather and distribute and connect."[2]

While messages have been accessible outside designated worship services for some time (messages on cassette, CD, etc.), it has never been this *easy* to access them—from our own churches and from hundreds, if not thousands, of others. As I look at the popular podcasts in the Christianity category, I can listen to messages from Lutherans, Methodists, Charismatics, Mormons, Reformed churches, nondenominational churches, Southern Baptists, seminary professors, fundamentalists, progressives, evangelical conferences, Presbyterians, Tim Keller, N. T. Wright.

People no longer need to go to church to hear the Word, which has been the selling point for local churches for the past fifty years. Because of this, church is becoming less of a possessor of knowledge (commodity) and more a communal hub.

WHY SHARING IS SO IMPORTANT

The new media culture is not just arriving, it's already here. We're living in a time when new media values are *presently ingrained* into an entire generation. Life will not "return to normal."

Wall Street Journal blogger Gary Hamel said in his lecture at the 2009 Leadership Summit, "The Facebook generation does not want to go to a church that feels like a corporation. They want a flexible community that has a cause—a cause that they can organically help create." Truthfully, isn't this the cry of every Christian's heart? Nevertheless, the need is alive and well in a new media culture.

To put this into context, imagine you're going overseas on a long-term missions trip. You do not speak the language, eat the foods, or dress in the same fashion as the folks in the culture you're heading to. In nearly every way, you are different from the environment you will soon find yourself immersed in.

If you're a good missionary, you'll begin to prepare well before your departure. You'll begin to study the language closely, picking up the conversational basics. You don't need to be fluent; you just need to be able to ask, "What did I just eat?" and "Where's the bathroom?"

You'll also want to have an idea of what's acceptable attire and what isn't. We have some missionary friends, Kevin and Erica, who serve in Pakistan. They knew the second they stepped on Pakistani soil that Erica's head would need to be covered. It was better for them to know this before they showed up than after. A small amount of cultural awareness went a long way to ensure their safety. Sharing in the cultural rhythms of your soon-to-be home isn't just a nice gesture, it's the key to your survival!

Lastly and most difficult, you'll want to have a general idea of the cultural mores, norms, and taboos. For instance, you should never touch anyone in India with your left hand. The left hand is used for one's "morning business" (if you catch my drift). In Japan, you don't stand up after a meeting until the person with the highest professional status does. If you ever come to Iowa and someone offers you sweet corn, don't you dare turn it down.

Good missionaries understand the culture they're called to serve. If you're reading this book, you are called to serve a digital culture. This culture operates differently than the one you might have grown up in. It's different from the one of just a few short years ago. This culture thinks, believes, buys, behaves, and speaks differently than any culture you may be familiar with. This cannot be overstated.

We need to rethink the way we interact with this digital culture. Sharing is a new way of life. There are no more one-way streets. Everything is participatory. A new media culture is not content to sit idly by.

THE DIGITAL KIMONO

Take Hudson Taylor, for example. Taylor was an American missionary to China in the late nineteenth century. He was a guy who thought and lived differently. He didn't just want to go and tell the gospel story to a group of people; he wanted to embody the life of Jesus in front of China. His mind was fixated on becoming a bridge—a relational line, if you will—between Jesus and the Chinese people.

This consuming desire led Taylor to think differently about the standard Western garb he was used to wearing. A dignified Westerner in this day wore a buttoned-up, three-piece suit and taught those around him to do the same. Westerners set the trends and expected others to follow "suit" (delicious pun intended). But not Taylor. I told you he was different. He understood one's cultural identity was closely tied to what one wore.

Think about it. Why are Texans always pictured wearing cowboy boots and ten-gallon hats? Certainly not every Texan has a pair of boots, but many do. It's part of the cultural fabric there. Similarly, if you were to visit Mumbai, India, you would see the majority of people wearing saris, sherwanis, and kurtas. There's a practical application—India is a hot country and these styles provide cooling relief from the oppressive heat. There's also a cultural application—these clothes provide appropriate coverage for both genders in a culture dedicated to modesty.

Hudson Taylor understood this dynamic in a way few missionaries have since. He knew cultural acceptance was, to some degree, dependent on looking like everyone else. As a white Westerner, he already had two very large strikes against him. Not one to be deterred, Taylor shucked the suit in favor of standard dress, something like a kimono. To be fully present to the Chinese people, Taylor began dressing like them. Genius. (If you want to see a picture of Hudson in his getup, go here: http://bit.ly/socialchurch-hudson.)

In one move, Taylor gained more cultural credibility than 100 years' worth of preaching ever could. As a good missionary, he knew he needed to speak the same language as the culture he was serving. By adopting the kimono instead of stubbornly holding on to his Western wardrobe, Taylor communicated, "I am here to learn from you, first and foremost. I have a message to share with you, yes. But I'm also here to learn. I want this to be a two-way street. You can trust me."

That kimono got Taylor into places he could never have dreamed, all for the sake of the gospel. The sheer audacity of someone wearing a piece of clothing reserved only for those on the "inside" was enough to gain an audience with even the most skeptical person in all of China. It was simple, it was absurd, and it got people to ask questions.

I believe we need to be more like Hudson Taylor. We need to look around and find the kimonos of our culture and start wearing them. Christians may not want to change the way that we do things. We may not want to change the way we've always looked. (I'm sure Hudson Taylor never said to himself, "Boy, these flowing silk robes sure make me look manly!") But we do it because of what it communicates to the people around us.

If you go to church next Sunday and the pastor gives his message in English, Scripture is read from an English translation, or people in the worship band are playing guitars, drums, or keyboards, you are the beneficiary of someone like Hudson Taylor. A long time ago, someone cared enough about you to translate the message of Jesus into a language you could understand. Someone said, "Hey, we should really think about giving this English thing a go." Simply put, someone went before you, put on a kimono, and got to work.

The "kimonos" of our culture are digital in nature. If we're going to communicate our message effectively, we need to know how to translate it into a language the culture around us can understand. I'm not talking about *changing* the message. I'm talking about changing the *way* we communicate it. This is something the church has always struggled with, but I'm convinced understanding this dynamic is more important than ever.

Practically speaking, it means we don't scoff at churches attempting to understand what it means to be a church online. It means we don't say ridiculous things like, "Jesus would never be on Facebook." Good grief. It means we don't look at social media as a "fad," instead seeing it for what it is: the biggest shift in the history of human communication.

Wearing kimonos isn't for shock value or novelty's sake. It's to show humility to a watching, waiting, weary world. A humility that says, "I want to tell you about someone who can change your life. I also want to see who you are, what makes you tick. Hopefully I can share the same. I'm not here to speak at you. I'm here to share my life with you."

Social media is disruptive. Every other societal building block has been disrupted by the shift toward social. Why would we think the church should be any different?

9

THE MEDIUM IS THE MESSAGE (AND THE MESSAGE DOESN'T CHANGE)

IT WAS EARLY SEPTEMBER and classes had just gotten under way. The classroom was hot, stuffy, and smelled of old books and body odor, which was especially surprising considering the entire building we were sitting in was brand-new. Equally surprising was the required course material for our class. It was my senior year, which meant I hadn't been buying books for the better part of twelve months. They cost too much, I never read the assignments anyway, and I hated standing in line. (We had to buy books the old-fashioned way back in 2001. An event that consisted of milling about the front door of the university bookstore, waiting for the doors to open on "book day," and sprinting to the section where you *hoped* your book would be. Even if you got a copy, it probably looked like it had been a chew toy for a dog living in a fraternity house. Amazon.com, as we know it now, was just a glimmer in the eye of Jeff Bezos.)

Wedged amongst the other seemingly irrelevant class readings was a book published in 1964, written by a Canadian philosopher of communication theory. The author's name was

Marshall McLuhan and the book was called *Understanding Media: The Extensions of Man*. I remember three things about my college education: (1) Learning about "the second shift" and resolving that my yet-to-be-named wife would never have to work it alone, (2) Lit firecrackers do not belong in porcelain toilets, and (3) This book. I remember it sharply, in fact. It had a far-reaching influence on me; I'm still unpacking the ways it shaped my thinking around how human beings communicate.

During the second or third class, a discussion evolved from one of the pages of McLuhan's book. Our professor leafed through the pages of her well-worn McLuhan copy and read aloud the words that have been haunting me ever since. Clearing her throat and speaking in the endearing accent that followed her from her days as a child in China: "The medium is the message."

IT'S NOT *WHAT* YOU SAY, IT'S *HOW* YOU SAY IT

The medium is the message. A statement that on the surface seems ridiculous and inane. What does it even mean? What medium? Which message? What's the relationship? This was too much for a class that met before my self-imposed "no classes before nine in the morning" policy. Nevertheless, my professor captured my attention and I was engaged.

If you haven't read the book, I don't necessarily recommend you do so. It's one of those reads that academic types gravitate toward, nestled up next to a fire, wearing a tweed jacket, and smoking a pipe.

The most important part of McLuhan's book is the aforementioned phrase and the implications it has for how we encode and decipher media. If the medium is the message, then how a message is conveyed must be considered, at least in some way, to be just as important as what the message is. It's not just *what* you say, but it's *how* you say it. McLuhan's theory (if you could call it that) posits the medium one uses to communicate a message changes the inherent meaning of the message.

Author and Dallas Theological Seminary staff member John Dyer says it best when explaining McLuhan for the Christian man or woman:

> Whether a person spends long periods of time reading Christian apologetics or spends that time reading atheist literature, the reader will increase the ability to understand complex arguments. And whether a person reads thousands of tweets from Ashton Kutcher and Britney Spears or thousands of tweets from John Piper and a C. S. Lewis robot, the skill of consuming massive amounts of small information bytes will increase.[1]

Regardless of *what* content we're reading, whether it be a tome or tweet, we're learning or strengthening a new way to process information. In the case of long-form literature, we gain the ability to engage an idea and follow it through the pages of a book (much like you're doing right now). With tweets (or status updates, blog posts, etc.), we teach ourselves how to add context to information that otherwise may leave us quizzical. (Think of this last example as the digital version of a disembodied head. If one happens upon a severed head—and I hope you never do!—most of us would understand the head came from *somewhere*. The head once belonged to a body with arms, legs, etc. Similarly, social media is teaching us to put the "arms" and "legs" on the disembodied information we come across on the web. For better or worse, by the way.) Dyer explains further,

In each of these cases [long-form reading or tweets], the effect of technology on the brain and body happen irrespective of the content. Of course, the content we consume is important, but often we focus so much on the content that we miss the importance of the medium through which we consume it. In fact, sometimes the effects of a medium are more important than any content transmitted through that medium.[2]

Again, *the medium is the message*. Every medium comes complete with an inherent meaning that we must seek to understand and be cognizant of. To not do so is to reverse the proper role humanity has with the technology we create (and every medium, from the paintbrush to the pencil to the pixel, is to be considered a technological advance). We abdicate that our discernment and technology literally begins to do our thinking for us. This, by the way, is the entire plot for the movie *The Matrix*. In fact, Mr. Smith, the computer program antagonist of the film, says at one point, "This really became our world (referring to the machines) when we started thinking *for you* (the humans)." Chilling! (Hear the call of Morpheus who says, "Free your mind."[3] It is only when we begin to understand the effect a medium has on us that we can truly begin to use it properly.)

Think of it this way: Writing a letter by hand creates a different end product than when you write the same note in an email. There is something about a handwritten note that conveys intentionality, love, kindness, and warmth that gets lost on a computer screen. A note is tangible, tactile, and carries with it some essence of the sender. (How many times have you seen someone's handwriting and thought, "This tells me everything I need to know about him/her!" Entire professions have evolved around analyzing handwriting, and for good reason. It reveals a great deal about a person.)

When I receive a handwritten note from my wife, in many ways it doesn't matter what it says. It could be a mundane grocery list, but so long as she writes my name somewhere and "Love, Kerry," I'm hooked. The note (the medium) signifies to my brain she loves and cares for me (the message) because she took the time to write by hand rather than hurriedly type it in an email. In a very real sense, the medium (the note) is the message ("I love you").

Let's put it in a different context. I know it's hard to imagine, but there was a time when the *only way* to receive a Bible was to wait years, sometimes decades, for a copy to be created by a monk. Even then, those copies came at a premium and often went to clergy. Monks used to copy what we know as the Bible word by word, line by line, not because they necessarily enjoyed doing so, but because it was the only way to preserve the written Word. You couldn't just walk down to your local Christian bookstore and pick from the myriad translations and surplus of study Bibles. Scripture came with a hefty price tag.

Did you ever have a teacher in high school who let you have a "cheat sheet" for a test? "Write all the notes you can on a 3x5 card, front and back, and bring it to the exam," they'd say. I'm here to tell you it was a trick. Your teacher knew that if you prepared for a test by filling up an index card with notes, you'd be reasonably prepared and probably wouldn't even need it. Your teacher got you to study, learn, and internalize the material without you even knowing it. People have different learning styles, but sitting with a subject in this manner leads to internalization that studying alone cannot equal. (Teachers, feel free to use this method in your class. You'll look like a hero *and* your students will do better on their tests. Promise.)

I'd like to think the same dynamic applied to the monks. As they sat, day after day, month after month, studying, writing, and repeating, their lives became enriched by the words they'd been charged to write. There was a richness, a depth, that the pages of Scripture had carved in their hearts. Writing Scripture is a multisensory activity. The monks felt the pressure of the writing instrument in their hand. They also saw the words on one page and copied each one to a different page, one by one.

While I certainly don't think we need to go back to writing out Scripture word for word, I do think we've lost something in translation. What our fragmented, social media-driven culture makes up for in speed and efficiency, we lose in richness and depth. If the medium is the message, writing by hand is the slow cooker and social media is the microwave.

JUICING, FIBER, AND HOW I ALMOST DIED

For instance, my wife and I got on a juice kick a little while ago. We bought a nice juicer and began juicing everything we could get our hands on. Beets, carrots, cucumbers, celery, oranges, lemons, limes, grapes—you name it, I'd juice it. (This included an ill-advised "salsa in a glass" episode involving the juice of tomatoes, onions, garlic cloves, and a jalapeño. If you want to see how fast your esophagus can constrict on itself, juice a jalapeño and drink it.)

Then there were apples. I loved juicing apples. I say "loved" because our chiropractor nearly banned me from juicing them after he learned how many I was consuming daily. Apples, along with many other fruits and vegetables, have "meat" (a.k.a. the stuff that's not juice) that aids in the digestion of the sugars present in the juice. In other words, an apple has its own regulation system built in. The time it takes you to eat an apple—bite, chew, swallow—gives the body time to process all the sucrose. When you juice an apple, you take the regulation system out of the equation, forcing your body to work overtime to process all the sucrose naturally present in fruit juices.

Writing by hand works much the same way. When we write things by hand, our mind is forced to slow down and process things at a much deeper level. Even the fastest hand-writer is no match for a decently skilled person typing on a computer.

Writing by hand is the "regulation system" it takes to deeply process our thoughts and present them in a cogent way. Typing on a computer removes the "regulation system" to a degree and allows us to process our thoughts faster. Sometimes this is beneficial—we're working on a deadline and need to have a proposal to a client immediately. Other times it's not—we want to get the greeting card for our parents' wedding anniversary *just right*.

It's not to say one is better than the other. We just need to be aware that the medium we choose to convey a message influences the message itself. As McLuhan himself said, "The personal and social consequences of any medium—that is, of any extension of ourselves—result from the new scale that is introduced into our affairs by each extension of ourselves or by any new technology."[4] To apply this in our earlier example, what we gain in efficiency by typing on a computer, communicating through social media we have the potential to lose the thoughtfulness that comes from writing a message by hand.

Volumes have been written about McLuhan's statement, so I won't continue to unpack what has been done elsewhere and in greater detail.[5] But a cursory understanding of McLuhan's principle is needed to see how it applies to churches in the twenty-first century. Understanding the mediums we use to communicate our message is critical.

When Martin Luther co-opted the printing press for the mass production of Bibles, it flattened the power structure of the entire church. An instrument of control, the printed Bible, was taken from the hands of those in power (i.e., the clergy). They no longer served as the sole source of spiritual guidance. People could read and understand God's Word for themselves for the first time in centuries.

The medium in this example—the printing press—gave us mass production of the Bible. But the underlying message, the one nestled below the truths of Scripture, was, at least initially, "You no longer need to be a helpless victim. The power is yours. The gatekeepers are gone." The intended consequence of this technology was that everyday, normal people could read the Bible for themselves. The unintended consequence was the revolution it sparked in the church. A revolution that led to many a needless death and a church split we still haven't healed from (Catholics vs. Protestants, anyone?).

This movement had both intended and unintended consequences; both helpful and hurtful. Helpful in that all people, regardless of their socioeconomic status, could get their hands on Scripture. Hurtful in the sense that, well, *everyone could get their hands on Scripture.* There is a benefit to having trusted spiritual leaders who dedicate their lives to the shepherding of God's flock, faithfully studying the Scriptures and leading the community in its interpretation. When you remove the gatekeepers, this can sometimes lead to a sort of vigilante interpretation of the Bible. Anyone who's been to a Bible study knows exactly what I'm talking about. We've all sat next to, or even been, the person who says, "That may be true for *you*, but it's not true for *me*." Sometimes gatekeepers are a good thing (until they're not).

BEING IN CHURCH VS. WATCHING CHURCH

To put this into a more modern context, churches need to consider the unintended consequences of live streaming their weekly worship services. (If you're not familiar with live streaming, think of it as television online. Churches will often put their entire worship service, from beginning to end, on their website, accessible by anyone in the world who has an Internet connection.) Live streaming gives us the opportunity to be a part of more church communities in one day than people fifty years ago could in a lifetime. My Twitter feed is literally filled with invites to online services on most Saturday nights and Sunday mornings.

Again, churches must be mindful of how the live-streaming environment (the medium) affects the worship service (the message). For instance, many pastors will greet the online viewing audience at the beginning of the service or before the message. This changes the relationship between the people who are physically present at the church building and the person delivering the message.

Practically speaking, it changes what it means to attend a worship service. Some churches who live stream services include online viewers in their weekly attendance figures; others do not. If someone watches a worship service online surrounded by friends and family, all of whom are participating, does this mean they "attended" church? Put crudely, does it "count"? If nothing else, it certainly brings a new meaning to Jesus' words, "Where two or three gather together as my followers, I am there among them."[6]

Our choice to engage (or not engage) online worship has implications for our churches. One glaring example is the underlying message of convenience. Anyone who's attempted to wrangle, pack up, and transport small children to and from church understands the challenge inherent in the task. As a father of young ones, there have been plenty of times where we've opted for our church's online service out of sheer exhaustion. Plus, there's something special about gathering your entire family for a worship service—just the four of you.

This season of our lives will pass. There will be a time when our children will sit through a service without vomiting and/or pooping on themselves; when they'll go to kids' church and come back with questions like, "Where is God?" and "Did the baby Jesus wear diapers?"; when they'll ask to go to youth group, see their friends, eat pizza, and do the things awkward teenagers do when someone from the opposite sex walks by. When these things happen, we probably won't have much need for the online service. But for right now, it's a lifesaver for our family. It allows us to maintain a connection with the communal goings-on of the church when we can't be there.

While I used to feel guilty about this, or like a "less-than" Christian, I've stopped feeling that way. Attending our church online has given me an entirely new perspective on what it means to "go" to church. Online services, coupled with a strong new media connection to our church, truly pave the way for a *new way* to be the church.

Yet there are some voices in Christendom who seek to dismiss online services outright because they do not match up with a certain paradigm of what does or does not constitute "church." At the risk of setting up a straw man, some believers are wary of online campuses because of the apparent loss of faith being embodied in a community. This is certainly an understandable objection, as Christianity is most decidedly a "team sport." But is our God not mighty to save? If the one who cannot be bound by space, time, the Red Sea, or our religion, if the one who speaks through deceivers, donkeys, and dead men, if God is the one who confounds death, surely he can find a way to speak through an Internet connection. Can he not?

Objections to online campuses (and new media in general) are most appropriate in the context of McLuhan's theory. We must understand and be mindful of the unintended messages embedded in the mediums we choose to communicate through. While I've laid out my personal convictions, this doesn't mean the privilege is not abused. It is frighteningly easy to opt for the PJs instead of getting ready for church and taking the entire family along with me.

In the midst of this discussion, we must remember the early church was built on the back of technology: St. Paul's letters. Practically speaking, the letters Paul wrote allowed him to be "present" in multiple places at once. And by "present" I certainly don't mean physically present. He was "present" in the sense the discipleship instructions contained in his letters led others to allow the Holy Spirit to produce fruit in their lives. When he was jailed and in handcuffs, sitting in a Roman prison, God was using Paul not only *inside* his jail cell, but across the entire region through his letters. Technology provided a presence for Paul and extended his reach when he could not be there physically.

As we've seen, Luther was able to send the Bible into the four corners of Germany (and eventually the world), giving millions access to the written Word of God. He used a medium to extend the presence of the Spirit's ministry, paving a way for it to go where it previously had not been (at least, not as prominently).

We laugh now, but televangelism, before it got goofy, was something quite extraordinary. The television acted as a medium for God's presence, beaming into homes.

Today, online campuses serve a similar purpose as the mediums of days gone by. Same with social networks, blogs, and websites. Each of these forums, together called an *online presence*, extend the reach of the church. They allow us to extend our reach into the lives of people we know, love, and care about. Because we are ambassadors of Jesus, his presence accompanies us into the nooks and crannies of the web. We are aware of this *presence extension* to some degree, but mostly we are blind to the extent that digital presence influences and affects the behaviors of others. Never underestimate the power of presence—online or off.

Online campuses that exist solely to increase the convenience quotient in one's life are detrimental and to be avoided at all costs. Online campuses are intended to facilitate connection to the church community, not replace it.

To the extent online campuses facilitate a connection between individuals and the Holy Spirit, they are beneficial and should be used whenever and however possible. But it's much like the old marketer's adage: "I'm wasting 50 percent of my marketing budget. The only problem is, I don't know which half!" As followers of Jesus, our responsibility is to sow seed as often as we can. The results, biblically speaking, are up to God and God alone.

BRIEF BITES

If "the medium is the message," digital communication comes with the in-built message of brevity. Online networks like Twitter, Pinterest, Tumblr, or Facebook are not built for long-form sharing. Twitter has a 140-character limit. Vine, the video version of Twitter, has a limit of six seconds. Online video viewership drastically drops at the two-minute mark. Facebook stands alone with a 63,206 character limit for statuses; however, statuses longer than two sentences are automatically truncated in the news feed. Pinterest, an image-based social network, grew their user base by 2,702 percent from May 2011 to January 2012. The incredible growth points to both the direction the web in general is going (e.g., image-based) and the network's ability to quickly present users with the information they want (If a picture is worth a thousand words . . .).

But brevity doesn't necessarily have to be a bad thing. The embedded message in a social media culture forces us to drill down into what is essential. We are compelled to ask the question, "What is absolutely necessary in this situation?"

Brevity doesn't need to imply skipping over critical information, either. Blaise Pascal is commonly cited as saying, "If I had more time, I would've written a shorter letter." To be brief is to be intentional. When we're bound by time to produce or create intended results, the chaff has a way of falling to the floor in an expedited fashion.

Jesus was brief. Brevity—or an intentional focus on the essentials—was a common theme throughout his ministry. Think of the key phrases that punctuate what we know of him:

"Follow me."[7]

"Love your enemies."[8]

"Do not judge others, and you will not be judged."[9]

"Do to others whatever you would like them to do to you."[10]

"Let the one who has never sinned throw the first stone."[11]

These are statements that convey an enormous amount of meaning in a few short words.

Any preacher or pastor who's had less than enough time to prepare a message understands the words of Martin Luther: "If I had my time to go over again, I would make my sermons much shorter, for I am conscious they have been too wordy."[12] When time is short, intentional thought is one of the first things to go.

CREATED TO COMMUNICATE

I agree with Neil Postman, a disciple of McLuhan, on this point. Postman says the goal of "the medium is the message" should be to help a society understand how media affects the broader culture. The danger behind technology—specifically behind technology related to digital communication—is when we become unaware (or, rather, remain unaware) of how a medium affects us. In a genius section of *Amusing Ourselves to Death*, Postman explains:

> I appreciate junk (television) as much as the next fellow, and I know full well that the printing press has generated enough of it to fill the Grand Canyon to overflowing. Television is not old enough to have matched printing's output of junk . . . we do not measure a culture by its output of undisguised trivialities but by what it claims as significant. Therein is our problem, for television is at its most trivial and, therefore, most dangerous when its aspirations are high, when it presents itself as a carrier of important cultural conversations.[13]

Postman is saying we need to call things what they are. Media has always been social. It has never existed as an end in and of itself. Stories have always been shared in one way, shape, or form, be it around the glow of a campfire or the glow of a computer screen. Human beings have persistently found ways to creatively share who they are and what they have created through the various mediums of history. Tribal stories shared around a campfire, smoke signals, ancient cave drawings depicting a hunt for food, the letters of St. Paul to the earliest churches, carrier pigeons, the Pony Express, Morse code, eight-tracks, cassette tapes, compact discs, digital video discs, Blu-ray, books, blogs, texting, tweeting, sharing, liking, infomercials. Heck, we're still sending radio signals 11 billion miles into space to communicate with *Voyager I*, which launched into space in 1977. *Voyager I*, in fact, has almost left the solar system.[14] We seem a species hard-wired for sharing. We literally cannot stop communicating. It is an inextricable part of who we are.

The first book of the Bible sheds light on why. Genesis tells the story of how Yahweh created humankind: "God created human beings in his own image. In the image of God he created them; male and female he created them."[15]

Human communication is so vital, so important, so essential to who we are, it is at the root of Original Sin. In Genesis 3, the Serpent tempts Eve with the siren song of, "Did God really say . . ." Eve takes the bait (we all would have, by the way) and the semantic battle begins. As Neil Postman wrote, "Speech . . . is the primal and indespensible medium. It made us human, keeps us human, and in fact defines what human means."[16] Preach.

JESUS' MEDIUM: THE TANGIBLE CHRIST

St. Paul writes in Ephesians about the significance of Jesus' humanity. He basically says to them, "Listen, I've given up everything to tell people about the life to be found in Jesus. I'm not sure why God chose me to share this message, but he did. So, here it is." Then, in what seems like a throw-away sentence, Paul says, "For this reason I bow my knees before the Father, from whom every family in heaven and on earth derives its name."[17]

See, the Ephesians were part of a little group called the Gentiles. If you're not familiar with the term, think of Gentiles as the table at the family reunion reserved for the weird uncles. No one can remember who they're actually related to, but you'd feel guilty for kicking them out. Gentiles (a.k.a. "outsiders") had it rough . . . until Jesus. Jesus erased the line between Jew and Gentile; between "accepted" and "rejected." In Ephesians 3, Paul plainly states how big of a deal this really is. Additionally, he was chosen as a messenger to the Gentiles to unpack the good news of Jesus Christ. Talk about worlds colliding!

This, dear readers, is the setting for this line of the letter, "from whom *every family in heaven and on earth derives its name*" (emphasis mine). Let's stop here because, although it may not seem like much, this is a very, very big deal. The word "family" Paul uses here is the Greek work *patria*, which comes from the word *pater*, or "father." In this context, *patria* signifies a family or tribe. It's a small word with huge implications.

Paul tells us the nature of family is found in God the Father. Paul declares the Gentiles are now a part of God's family. Jesus is the firstborn—the role model—of this new brood. In a different letter to a Roman church, Paul says, "God knew his people in advance, and he chose them to become like his Son, so that his Son would be the firstborn among many brothers and sisters."[18]

What does the "medium" of Christ teach us about God? If media have an explanation and an essence (i.e., the "real message"), what do we learn about God in the person of Jesus Christ?

First, the most obvious and prominent medium is the flesh-and-blood body of Christ. In his wisdom, God the Father could have chosen to present his Son to the world in a myriad of ways.

Literally, anything we can conceive (and much of what we can't) was (and still is) available to God to convey the message of the Christ. Angels, archangels, cherubim, seraphim, the animal kingdom, all of nature, the stars, moon, sun, and beyond—God could have chosen to present himself in all of these things. But he didn't. He chose to inhabit—literally dwell within—a human body. "For God in all his fullness was pleased to live in Christ."[19]

But why a body? Why flesh? Why blood? What do these mediums tell us? Why did God choose to appear in a "medium" that is clumsy and vulnerable? A medium that breaks down so easily and tires so quickly?

In case you haven't noticed, our bodies are not impenetrable. I proved this to myself just last night as I firmly planted my foot on one of my son's surprisingly sharp action figures. Words cannot express the pain felt by an acutely accurate jab to one's foot meat. Our bodies have a resolve and possess the ability to rebound when given enough time, but they're also vulnerable.

Jesus is the fulfillment of the image bearer identity we all have inherently instilled in us by God the Father. He is the perfect human—what a life lived infused with the Holy Spirit looks like. He is, quite literally, the Alpha example of a life devoted to the purposes and plan of God. This, my friends, is the essence of the good news.

When we see Jesus, we see a man who possessed a deep capacity to embrace what it means to be human. We see him celebrating at weddings, deeply mourning the death of a friend, enraged with anger at injustice, dining and enjoying the company of good friends, seeking solace when the crowd has become too much. This was not some stoic, unchanging robot deity with no capacity for emotional breadth. No, this was a fully God, fully man who embodied the very God-breathed essence of how to be human.

My favorite example highlighting the humanity of Jesus comes in the garden of Gethsemane. It's quite fitting that humanity's origin begins in a garden and here, in a different garden, we see fully God, fully man coming to grips with the very purpose for which he was created: death.

The Gethsemane story appears in three of the four gospels, but none do it justice like Luke. Luke, a meticulous, fact-minded doctor, writes with the purpose of emphasizing the humanity of Christ—more so than any other gospel. He presents the raw emotion of Jesus' agony in a way that leaves the reader breathless. It is impossible to read Luke's account of Gethsemane and walk away unchanged.

In chapter 22, Luke writes about an intimate moment Jesus has with his Father: "Father, if you are willing, please take this cup of suffering away from me." It's easy to gloss over this sentence without fully realizing the implications. They are, in a word, astounding. This may be obvious to you, but do you realize what Jesus is asking for here? He's praying to have the perverse punishment that awaits him on the cross to be removed. He does not want to do it. He's pleading—begging—with his Father to achieve the redemption of humankind another way.

If you grew up going to Sunday school, this may come as a shock to you. I know it did for me. We always picture Jesus as a perpetually good-tempered person who wears sweater vests and drinks Yoohoo. He's always in a good mood, even when dragging his own execution device behind him. Even when he's nailed to the cross, Sunday school Jesus sees the pain as a mild discomfort—like having to pay your taxes or serve jury duty.

Yet, the Bible gives us a much different picture than Sunday school Jesus. Matthew shows us a dialogue between Jesus and some of the disciples, wherein he confesses, "My soul is crushed with grief to the point of death."[20] Mark's version of Gethsemane reveals Jesus crying out for his *Abba*,[21] or quite literally, "Daddy." (As a father, Mark's narrative pierces my heart in a unique way.)

Then, of course, there is Luke crafting the narrative to include one of the most profound sentences in all of Scripture, "He (Jesus) was in such agony of spirit that his *sweat fell to the ground like great drops of blood*"[22] (emphasis mine). It is unclear whether the sweat falling from Jesus' face was actually red in color, like blood (there's a medical term for it called *hematidrosis*), or he was sweating so profusely it resembled blood cascading from an open wound. When you add up the different vantage points from Matthew, Mark, and Luke, you see a man who was struggling so intensely with his God-given calling—his purpose—it literally felt like he was dying.

But what was Jesus' response to the Father's call? Presumably while in prayer, Jesus received the answer he was hoping to avoid. The call was clear: the cross was set before him and it was a path he must travel. In the face of this unflinching assignment, Jesus responds impeccably, saying, "I want your will to be done, not mine."[23] He submits his plans, purposes, and preferences to the Father in an ultimate act of trust, faith, and obedience.

What does the medium of "being human" reveal about God? What's the "essence" of being human? If we reflect his image, there must be characteristics we can learn about *Jehovah-Jireh* by observing humanity. When you look at a watch, for instance, you learn something about the watchmaker. A watch is incredibly intricate. Therefore the maker must have a keen eye for detail, patience for ensuring all the gears and springs work correctly, and wisdom to know the difference between a winding pinion and wheel pivot.

As we have already seen, Jesus is the quintessential human. He is the fulfillment of what Creator God intended in the garden of Eden. Jesus' death and resurrection ensure that we, as his brothers and sisters, have access to the life we were intended to live through a relationship with him. When we look at Scripture, we see the bodily metaphor everywhere. The metaphor is around every corner, primarily in the New Testament.

This is for a reason. We are God's body on earth because Jesus was.

Jesus is God's way of saying, "You are not alone."

As digital ambassadors, we're enabled to go out into all the world and bring others the life they were intended to live. We can span great gaps and tell the world, "you're not alone." It is time to grasp what an embodied gospel looks like in a digital world. We must adapt our methods without changing the message.

TO WHOM SHALL WE GO?

New wine must be stored in new wineskins.

LUKE 5:38

10

PYRAMIDS AREN'T JUST IN EGYPT

THE MAJORITY OF COMMUNICATION issues boil down to not having a Big Idea. A Big Idea is what gets you out of bed in the morning. It's why you do what you do every day. It has to extend beyond a mission statement on a placard somewhere nobody notices or thinks about.

A church's Big Idea has to be something you live and breathe and embody as a community.

Oftentimes when I talk to folks, I hear the same complaints:

- We aren't getting the click-throughs that we want on our emails.

- We aren't seeing the results we want from social media.

- We aren't getting the hits we want on our blog.

- What is THE DEAL?

These common problems most always revolve around the lack of a Big Idea. Now, people inside Big Idea-less organizations may say they know what their Big Idea is—especially in churches. It usually sounds something like, "Our Big Idea is to do *this* and to do *that* for all people everywhere under the sun while playing hopscotch and saying the alphabet backward." Throw in a few references to the gospel or to Jesus or to the nations, and you've got the Big Idea for nearly every church in America.

A Big Idea isn't something you just put on a plaque and place on a wall, or put on a company letterhead and let it sit there gathering dust. It shouldn't just be tucked nicely into the weekend bulletin or sit placidly on the sign out in the church's front lawn.

The Big Idea cannot be "to get a paycheck." That's a lousy Big Idea. Financial rewards, especially in younger generations, are lousy motivators. Frankly, they don't translate well into the other levels of the Wise Strategy Pyramid, which we'll discuss later in this chapter.

It should also be noted there are two types of application for a Big Idea, both internal and external. A Big Idea must first be embraced by the internal stakeholders (staff, pastors, executives, etc.) within an organization before it can be cemented in the psyche of the external stakeholders (church members, donors, volunteers, etc.). The psalmist wrote, "Oil flows from the head . . . down."[1] Never has this been truer than with the Big Idea!

JESUS' BIG IDEA

If ever there was a Big Idea, it was the one held by Jesus of Nazareth. Both fully God and fully man, Jesus didn't circumvent the process of living as a real, flesh-and-blood, breathing, eating, sleeping human being. He subjected himself to the same laws of physics, gravity, and vision you and I are constrained to.

He also showed us what can happen when a vision is fully submitted to God the Father. Jesus states plainly, "The Son can do nothing by himself. He does only what he sees the Father doing."[2] In other words, his Big Idea is going *nowhere* unless the Father breathes on it and gives it life.

Of course, you know how the story goes. Jesus dreamt of a world where brokenness, despair, pain, heartbreak, and futility didn't have the last word. He dreamt of a world where freedom, grace, goodness, and truth reigned supreme. He envisioned a world where you and I were restored to the dignified place in God's creation we once held in the garden. This was, and continues to be, the Big Idea held by the Spirit-filled carpenter from Nazareth.

When we see how Jesus communicated his Big Idea, it's clear it was heavily influenced by the power of narrative. He told stories that were easy to understand. His stories had an edge to them. After hearing Jesus speak, most folks walked away with plenty of questions. (*He's going to do what? On a what? For who? Me?!*)

The model Jesus used (invented?) looked like this:

1. Is the Big Idea simple?
2. Is the Big Idea absurd?
3. Does it get people to ask questions?

So that you don't think I'm a total heretic, here's a helpful example to contextualize our Big Idea formula.

A woman lost a valuable coin (simple premise). She looked all over to find it. (Absurd concept—*absurd* meaning out of the ordinary. This would be like turning your house inside-out for a twenty-dollar bill.) When she finally found it, she was super happy and told people about it (Why was she so happy about finding the coin? Further, why did she tell everyone about it?).

Big Idea: You're the coin. God is the lady. You matter to God. (That's Luke 15:8–10, by the way.)

Sounds good, right? Jesus was simple. His Big Idea is simple. But neither is simplistic.

Also, Jesus did not play it safe. He did not go around, preaching quietly, carefully forming his words so as to not offend anyone. In perhaps what is simultaneously one of my favorite passages and one that fills me with dread, Jesus says, "I have come to set the world on fire, and I wish it were already burning!"[3] Nothing neutral about that, is there?

I imagine the hearers of Jesus' message stomping away in anger, infuriated by what he said. (So angered, in fact, they started plotting how to end his life.)[4] Others were confused, elated, mystified, encouraged, or a mixture of all four. Jesus knew how to draw a crowd and we, as his followers, could stand to learn something from his model of absurdity.

The Bible is rife with absurdity: A prophet (Ezekiel) forced to eat his own excrement? A talking donkey (Balaam's, um, mule)? A man (Peter) finding money in a trout's mouth? These things are absurd. Yet each one was terribly effective at conveying the message God intended for the situation. Each story (and many others) weave a grander Big Idea throughout the Bible.

God's absurdity is purposeful. People gravitate toward extremes. The folks who stand tepidly in the middle tend to get overlooked and ignored. Jesus was neither. Put simply, "absurd" means to let your convictions guide you and pick a freaking side.

It also gets people to ask questions and stay engaged, just as everything Jesus said and did caused people to ask questions and keep following him around, seeing what he would say next.

We'll use this framework to lay out an approach you can take to start building a Big Idea (or improving on the one you already have). It works by giving the basic details and then enticing the imagination to fill in the gaps.

The Big Idea is so critical to establish because, without it, everything (and I mean *everything*) you're trying to communicate will be clouded by confusion. It'll lack the sharpness you need to cut through the clutter—everything from a mission statement to the weekly bulletin to a lowly tweet.

IS YOUR BIG IDEA SIMPLE?

If people aren't resonating with your current Big Idea, they don't need more rationale. It's not details they're after. More information isn't going to fill in the gaps. People need to be enticed. A compelling Big Idea allures people:

- *The Matrix*: There is no spoon.[5]

- Jesus: My purpose is to give [you] a rich and satisfying life.

- Mr. Rogers: Won't you be my neighbor?

- Southwest Airlines: Democratizing the skies with affordable travel.

Unlike these simple Big Ideas, churches unnecessarily turn their Big Ideas into elaborate labyrinths, fraught with complications around every turn. It's like a bad game of hokey-pokey that never ends. Have you ever visited or worked for a church with a Big Idea like this:

We exist . . .
To share the love of Christ . . .
With all people, everywhere, in all places . . .
So that the world may know . . .
And believe . . .
And be baptized . . .
And repent . . .
And be baptized while repenting . . .
On Tuesdays . . .

With Morrie . . .

To go into the nations . . .

And make disciples . . .

Of all nations . . .

While nation-ing . .

The nations about nations . . .

. . . then you shake it all about.

ACK!

If we don't complicate our Big Ideas grammatically, we do it socially. Case in point: What would your church do if someone showed up on Sunday morning in full drag? Would that person be welcomed into the community? Encouraged to join a small group? I think we all know the answer.

The best Big Ideas are simple. They clearly communicate how one can get involved while showing the benefit of participation. Effective Big Ideas motivate people in the community to show up every day and get involved. They're what resonate in the collective organizational gut. A compelling Big Idea keeps people coming back for more.

Here are some helpful questions to ask when determining your Big Idea:

1. What do the people in leadership bring to the table? Life experiences? Expertise? Was your senior pastor a former member of the Amish community? Does the communications director have a background in the corporate world? Did an associate pastor have a former life as a successful conference director? Use it. All of it.

2. What are we passionate about as a community? Do any themes come up over and over again?

3. Do the people within the community come to us for certain needs? Do we have an affectionate nickname in the

community? For example, one church leader told me at a conference that her congregation is known as "the hot dog church" because every Sunday during the summer, the church holds a giant cookout for people in the community. This event has led to a full-blown "meals for the homeless" program operated by the church. Feeding those in need has become central to this church's Big Idea.

4. Are you a denominational leader? How do you fit into the larger denominational structure? The church where I used to be on staff is a part of the Evangelical Lutheran Church in America (ELCA). It also happens to be the largest ELCA church in the country. Our size has led to some profound opportunities to shape the conversation within the denomination.

5. Lastly, what do you want to be *known* for? Your church's legacy is largely dependent on a cogent, clear, compelling Big Idea. How do you want to be remembered in the church universal?

There's a local church where I'm from that's known as the "adopting" church. It's how they're known in the community. Several people in the church have been adopted, and several others have adopted children of their own. So they've dialed in to what they're passionate about and owned it as their identity. They offer adoption classes and trainings. Their leaders have carefully discerned what they feel God has called them to do as a local congregation and used it to fuel their Big Idea.

A simple Big Idea is specific to the community and the people within it. In other words, it should be engaging enough to appeal to an outsider yet border on nonsensical to those who don't participate actively in the church community. It's a tricky balance, but it can (and should) be done.

Your organizational Big Idea has to be something that excites passion in you to do the work that you're doing. Otherwise, you're wasting time—yours and everyone else's. Make your Big Idea dead simple. Make your communication surrounding the Big Idea even simpler. More people will be engaged.

IS YOUR BIG IDEA ABSURD? DOES IT BEG FOR QUESTIONS?

Oftentimes in churches, our Big Ideas are founded around what I call "OAFAPs," which, of course, is short for "Offend as Few as Possible." OAFAPs are dangerous because they sound nice and flowery ("We want to save the whole world with heartwarming kazoo renditions of 'Kumbaya'!"), but they don't mean anything. No one sweats or bleeds or cries coming up with an OAFAP. While I'm not suggesting we intentionally go and pick fights, I think churches could stand to pick a side now and again.

One of my favorite examples of anti-OAFAPisms comes from East Lake Church in Chula Vista, California. After some nearby shark attacks (no one was seriously injured . . . I don't think), the good folks at East Lake put up signs in the local mall stating, "Sharks not welcome at East Lake Church."

That's hilarious—and absurd. And most likely a little offensive. But humor played a large role in the church's Big Idea. The "shark warning signs" had service times and locations on them, inviting passersby to church. Not everyone appreciated the jest, but it got people to check East Lake out. That's a great use of a Big Idea. And it gets people to ask questions about you and want to follow you around, waiting to see what your next move will be.

WHY COMMUNICATING *YOUR* BIG IDEA MATTERS

If the Big Idea isn't present—if it's not simple, absurd, and doesn't get people to ask questions—it's going to be very hard to communicate *anything* well.

Today, many churches are feeling the pain of not understanding how to put social media to work. How to use it effectively for organizational purposes. Church leaders have recognized social media isn't a fad. It's not going away. Even if leaders don't understand it, the tide has turned and social media is here to stay. (If that's news to you, or you're having a hard time believing what I just said, Google "Gary's social media count." Yeah. Those numbers will only keep increasing faster, by the way.)

If a church (or any organization, for that matter) attempts to create a social media strategy with an absent or unclear Big Idea, the results are usually disastrous. It's actually pretty tragic. An effective social media strategy is a by-product of a clear and compelling Big Idea.

Your church gets a Facebook page or a Twitter account or some other social media account *du jour*. "Hooray!" you think to yourself. "We're finally getting with the times!" says another staff member. As a social media advocate, you're rejoicing you finally have a chance to prove everyone wrong and show, once and for all, social media *does* work.

You eagerly get to work, setting up all the pages and accounts and URLs. Content seems to fly off your fingertips. It's effortless. Church members are flocking to your official accounts like moths to a flame. It's like an engagement bonanza! +1! Like! Retweet! Pin! Comment! The rush of social proof is intoxicating. You think, "How could this get any better? I'm winning at work and life! Jenga!"

Then, as I like to say in my wedding sermon while standing in front of a blushing bride and rugged groom, "The rose-colored glasses come off." You realize, quickly, social networks are not self-servicing. They're like those annoying Tamagotchi pets from the nineties. You know, the "virtual" pets you had to feed (virtually) or they would get sick and (virtually) die. Social networks need content to survive, otherwise they starve and die.

After such a strong start, content fatigues sets in. Accounts go days, weeks, even months with no updates. Virtual ghost towns. What started with such promise is now a withered, dry shell of social engagement entropy.

Okay, I may be pushing this analogy a bit, but we've all felt the pain of realizing, "Oh man, I gotta *take care* of these social networks?" They don't update themselves. But they stand a much a better chance at achieving desired results if there's a Big Idea for your strategy to rest on.

When there's no Big Idea to connect your social media strategy to, your social networks get blamed for a lack of results. People within your organization who don't understand the true value of social media may say it doesn't work, which is akin to blaming a shovel for not digging a deep enough hole. It's not the shovel's fault for not digging deep—it's the one wielding the shovel. It's simply a tool in the user's hand. Social media, in a practical sense[6], requires a skilled user to harness its true power.

A STARTING POINT FOR YOUR BIG IDEA

If you're feeling this tension between social media and your Big Idea, you're in good company. If you're wondering where to start, use this question as a jumping-in point for clarifying or creating your Big Idea: "What objectives are we trying to accomplish as a community?"

We have to start from the beginning. This one single question will form the bedrock for your Big Idea. When you can clearly state what you're trying to achieve, everything else seems to naturally fall into place.

Once you have a Big Idea, you're able to establish goals from your Big Idea, and that's how resources get allocated. Yep, I'm going to say the "B" word: Budget. It strikes fear into the heart of every kingdom-minded church worker across the world. Why? When we talk about allocating budget dollars, the waters can get a little, shall we say, choppy.

But budgeting doesn't have to be a painful process. When the Big Idea is clear, internal stakeholders can point to it and get leaders on all sides of the table on board with changes that embody the mission. (Establishing a Big Idea also has the added benefit of ferreting out any interpersonal conflicts. If any issues lurk beneath the surface, they have a way of bubbling up and out when mission and budget get discussed!)

For example, to focus on communicating better to teens and young adults, one church I worked with said, "We're going to cut our print budget by 15 percent and create a texting budget instead." This community's Big Idea was squarely focused on creating an atmosphere the youth in their city felt drawn to. This clear connection facilitated a change in budget to accomplish one of their goals via social media (and let's face it, texting is the mother of all social mediums!).

Or maybe you can reallocate resources to build and maintain a functional website. In one survey, 47 percent of respondents said a church's website actually factored into their decision-making process on whether or not to attend the church.[7] (That number will continue to climb, by the way.)

If enough people start asking the right kinds of questions, change will start to happen. It isn't going to happen overnight, but perhaps the shift in the culture of communication is actually giving us an opportunity to look at something deeper— the vision and the mission of our churches. Maybe we've taken the "why?" for granted for so long we've forgotten how to communicate it to a new generation.

Churches that choose not to evolve and change to keep up with shifting culture will simply go away. Not with a bang, but with a sad whimper. They will become moot relics in a culture that demands change and adaptation.

From a business perspective, this is why you see places like Blockbuster go bankrupt and disappear. Why? Because the folks at Blockbuster believed they were too big to fail. They were drunk on profits and dulled to the boiling waters slowly bubbling up around them. The situation reflects the words written in 1 Thessalonians, "When people are saying, 'Everything is peaceful and secure,' then disaster will fall on them as suddenly as a pregnant woman's labor pains begin. And there will be no escape."[8] And for Blockbuster, there wasn't.

Companies like Netflix swooped in between 2004–2009 and ate Blockbuster's lunch. Netflix had a business model that met people where they were—at home! Netflix customers got their DVDs (and eventually streaming video) delivered right to their doorstep. Suddenly, piling the fam' into the station wagon and rolling down to the local Blockbuster seemed like an archaic piece of Americana, like not having indoor plumbing. Blockbuster tried to play catch-up and offer the same type of services as Netflix, but it was too late. The damage had been done. The company filed for bankruptcy in 2010 and was sold to Dish Network in 2011 for a paltry $320 million. The irony in all of this is back in 2000, Blockbuster declined several offers to purchase Netflix for $50 million[9] (a drop in the bucket, considering how much Netflix was raking in even back then).

Lesson: Blockbuster didn't adapt their business model until it was too late, so they're not around anymore. I think churches who fail to adapt will probably suffer similar fates. They just won't be around. It is a misconception to believe that because you are a church you cannot fail. You can, and many do. Every year 3,500 churches close their doors.[10] Not every church that closes shop has failed to adapt, but many have.

The North American church is at a crossroads. We have a choice to make. We can go one direction, or another. Crudely speaking, we can be a Blockbuster—content with our current circumstances, avoiding the changing culture emerging around us, or we can be a Netflix—finding new ways to deliver a familiar message.

Church leaders and congregations need to answer many questions. Questions like:

- How do we go about finding the unique message of our local church and then translating that message to an online atmosphere?

- What does that look like?

- How do we build our church, God's kingdom, using social media?

- How do we fully express ourselves and tell our story through Twitter, Facebook, Pinterest, YouTube, our church website?

An important point we need to remember is there are people and churches excelling in the digital space, excelling in the digital communication. What we need to do is not pretend like it's impossible, and instead learn from those people and bring those lessons to the churches where we are.

BUILDING ON YOUR BIG IDEA

The Big Idea of your organization is crucial because it serves as your base. If you think of your communications strategy as a pyramid, your Big Idea sits at the bottom. It's the biggest part, the part that everything else rests upon.

The next level of the pyramid is going to be your content marketing strategy. Simply put, this is how you communicate the Big Idea, both internally and externally. Internally to staff, pastors, key volunteers, and other leaders. Externally to the congregation, community, and potential church members.

Your content strategy is the way you tell your church's story. As we'll see, this has implications for the information you place on your website, how it's structured and organized, the pictures you place on the website, what social networks you engage, and the tone of your online voice. In other words, it all matters.

Practically speaking, your content strategy includes print items like bulletins, brochures, table tents, posters, postcards, ministry magazines, registration forms, or any printed signage. It also includes digital items like emails, brochures, webinars, apps, podcasts, blogs, articles, white papers, images, infographics, music, animations, slide shows, videos, or even interactive games. For our purposes, we'll be focusing on the digital side of things.

Your content strategy will never work unless it rests on the big idea. Because, again, you take your Big Idea and develop a strategy for telling people, both inside and outside the organization, who you are and what your story is through the mediums I mentioned earlier.

This is where many churches get the order wrong. If you don't know why you exist—your Big Idea—it makes it very difficult to communicate that purpose through your content.

Take my friend Johanna, for instance. Johanna is the Communications Director at Eagle Brook Church in the Twin Cities. Outside of a general content strategy for the church, Johanna and her team develop separate content strategies for all major community-focused events. Each strategy includes:

- Medium/Platform: How are we going to tell the story?
- Target Audience: Who are we telling the story to?
- Estimated Cost: How much is telling the story going to cost?
- Info to Know: What do other people on staff need to know about the story we're telling? How can they contribute and make it better?

Everyone within the church is a communicator. Whether it's the facilities staff, the senior pastor, or the Sunday school teacher, they're all saying something about the culture of the church they represent. A dirty nursery speaks volumes to a parent and will determine whether or not a family comes back—more than a sermon ever could. A content strategy transcends weekly bulletins and signage. Every font choice, website stock photo, bathroom sign, every hole in the wall, even the beans a church chooses for the free church coffee—they all communicate something. The content strategy can help you determine whether or not you like what these elements are saying.

There must be a plan for reiterating the Big Idea over and over again to the church staff and key leadership. In turn, these folks need to be included in the plan to reiterate the Big Idea outside of the organization. Andy Stanley says, "Vision leaks." So you need to figure out ways to stop the leakage, to plug up the holes in the vision bucket. That is part of your content strategy.

Put simply, content is the new currency. Content is the language of a digital culture. It's how your vision is communicated. Without content, nothing else will work.

BUILDING ON TOP OF YOUR BIG IDEA: WEBSITE STRATEGY

Your Big Idea serves as the base for your content strategy. Your content strategy is the base for your website strategy.

Author and blogger Chris Brogan develops this thought quite a bit. He often references your website as your home base. It is the only portion of the Internet that you can own entirely. Every pixel on your website is and needs to be owned by you. This means *you* take responsibility for everything on your church's website. Often times this is where the bottleneck happens.

If your home base is cluttered, convoluted, or cringe-worthy, if people go to your website and don't know who you are, what you do, how to find you, or what gets you out of bed in the morning, they're going to go elsewhere and find another church that does know. They're going to look for a church that's done the hard work of finding out what their Big Idea is and how to communicate it clearly.

In working with dozens of churches over the past several years, I see many churches that fall victim to the Stock Photo syndrome. It's like the Stockholm syndrome, but instead of feeling empathy for your captors, you become enamored with dreadful, generic stock photos. A church with Stock Photo syndrome (SPS) has a website with nice stock photos of an incredibly diverse population where everyone is attractive, young, and laughing. All the time.

Churches with SPS have one problem: none of the photos they use represent the true environment of their church! If you were to go to a church website with SPS and then visit the church on a Sunday morning, it wouldn't look like what you expected. It's like the ultimate bait-and-switch. You'd look around and think, "Am I being punk'd? Where's Ashton Kutcher?" Websites not tethered to a Big Idea fall victim to SPS more often than not.

Another symptom of no Big Idea? The Info Dump. Websites with no purpose often become a receptacle for all the information no one really knows what to do with anymore. It's the online version of a junk drawer. You know, the drawer in every home where you put dried out pens, super glue, stamps, Matchbox cars, old keys, and all that other junk you can't quite figure out what to do with.

Churches with an Info Dump don't do the hard work of asking the question: "Should this go on our website?"

Should this event from five years ago still be on our calendar? Why is it still there? Who was responsible for taking it down? Is the information on the site clearly communicating who we are as an organization? Is it necessary to anyone else or just the staff member who put it there? Info Dumps also play well into the *Field of Dreams* phenomenon: "If I can just get my event or announcement on the website, people will magically come!" Wrong, wrong, wrong. On so many levels. Maybe people aren't coming to your event because it's poorly conceived and doesn't meet a real need in the community.

If you can't answer those questions with a reasonable sense of certainty, the content doesn't need to go on your website. If you have answers, you need a process for building content into the website so it accurately reflects your Big Idea. Then, make sure you have a process to keep your content from growing stale—someone's got to own each section. Do you have answers in place for these questions? If not, your website will never be as effective as it could be.

Count with me: 1 - 2 - 3 - 4 - 5 - 6 - 7. An average visitor will look at a website for seven to twelve seconds upon first visit. You have the time it takes sing "Happy Birthday" to capture someone's attention before they decide to go elsewhere. That's not a lot of time. To make the most out of these literal moments, do the hard work of connecting your website to your Big Idea. Remember, your website is the church home base. Does it accurately reflect who you are as a church or ministry? Does it tell the story of who you are as an organization?

BUILDING ON TOP OF YOUR BIG IDEA: SOCIAL MEDIA STRATEGY

Finally, after you've established your foundational Big Idea, after you've built a content strategy, and after you've done the hard work of connecting your website to your Big Idea, you get to the cherry on top. That cherry is the social media strategy for your organization.

A good social media strategy is the culmination of all the hard work you've been doing in the building this pyramid. Social media doesn't drive the strategy, it supplements the strategy. In other words, if you don't have a Big Idea, if you don't have a content marketing strategy, if you don't have a website strategy, your social media strategy isn't going to do a darn thing! Social media has to point back to your home base.

Social media seems to be an easy point of entry for many church leaders because it's where they're feeling the most pain. What's more immediately irritating: a paper cut between your thumb and forefinger (*yowch!*) or cancerous cells growing within your body? Of course, the paper cut hurts more in the here-and-now but is relatively harmless in the long run. I think we'd all agree cancer is much more deadly to someone's long-term health, but you don't necessarily feel acute pain from cancer like you would a paper cut.

An organization in need of an effective social media strategy usually wants for something deeper: a Big Idea. Starting with questions like, "How do we get more likes on our fan page?" or "Why doesn't anyone follow us back on Twitter?" is like putting a Band-Aid on a gaping flesh wound. It just doesn't make sense.

You don't need retweets; you need triage. You can buy likes. You can buy followers. Building an audience is the easy part. What's not easy is purposefully building each level of the communications pyramid.

In my experience, I find when a church *starts* with social media, it only compounds the problems found in the foundational levels of the communications pyramid. By way of example, did you see the horrific injury sustained by Louisville Cardinal Kevin Ware during the 2013 NCAA March Madness men's tournament? If you didn't, here's a summary: it was gross. Like, super gross. To give you an idea of the horrific nature of his injury, grown men began wailing like a newborn baby after seeing it. One of Ware's teammates began vomiting immediately. America cringed. It was bad.

The official diagnosis was a compound fracture, but anyone needing a doctor to tell them what they just saw would be surprised to learn the grass is green and sun is hot (there was bone sticking out, for Pete's sake!). Doctors said there wasn't a single cause for the fracture. It was a combination of tiny, hairline fractures, bone spurs, and landing at the wrong angle at the wrong time. It was the perfect storm.[11]

For our purposes, the same thing happens with church social media strategies. A weak social media strategy stems from not having an effective home base (i.e., a church website). In other words, you don't have a system in place to usher the conversation from the foyer to the living room. The website is a mess because there's no interwoven content strategy in place to tell the story of the Big Idea. Often, this is because there is no Big Idea—or at least a tepid, weak, or bland Big Idea. (Gentle reminder: effective Big Ideas are specific to the context of a local church; they're simple, absurd, and they get people to ask questions.)

I've seen churches with literally dozens of Facebook pages. Every ministry, every group, every department, every service feels the need to start their own page, sometimes just because they can. The youth group gets a page so men's ministry starts a page. The Underwater Basket Weavers ministry doesn't like what's going on with the main church page, so they grab their own fan page and start posting away. No one's in charge of directing the social stream, therefore *everyone* is in charge. That, my friends, is a recipe for disaster.

The main problem with this approach is having absolutely no strategy involved. No cohesive rhyme or reason for creating all these social networks. It's quite literally a digital landgrab.

Chris Brogan talks a lot about how social media are like your outposts. They point people back to your digital home, which is your website. So if your social media strategy is not aligned with those things, it won't work as well as it should. When I say working as it "should," I mean every social network you are on must have four things to work:

1. A development plan. How are you going to ensure there is a steady stream of content for each channel?
2. A voice. How is this social network going to express the voice of your Big Idea?
3. An owner. Who is going to take the reins of each specific social network. Name them.
4. A goal. How is each social medium you're participating in tied to an organizational goal?

Being on a social network can't be an end in and of itself; otherwise it fails.

You have to ask yourself, Does my organization have alignment in all four of these areas? Is our Big Idea aligned with our content strategy? Is our content strategy fueling our website strategy? Finally, is our website strategy forming a solid home base for the outposts in our social media strategy?

If so, hooray! Keep doing it. Keep working it. Keep ensuring those things have alignment.

Just like your car might get out of alignment after a rough winter or after you've driven it for a while, strategy can get out of alignment. Strategy consistently needs to be readjusted.

If you don't have alignment in the communications pyramid, consider it priority *numero uno*. Get each level synced up and formulated and put on paper. Get the troublemakers of your organization all in the same room, gather them around the same table, and hash these things out.

It is mission critical for your church to do these things and to do them well. Your future effectiveness as a kingdom-building community depends on it. Remember, establish the Big Idea, build a content strategy that answers the question, "How are we going to share our Big Idea?" Then, work your way toward a helpful website and interactive media strategy. You'll be well on your way to sharing your God-given mission with the world.

11

WASHING FEET

DO YOU HAVE A movie you're embarrassed to admit you enjoy?

The Twilight Saga?

Encino Man?

Teen Wolf? (Or the much-anticipated, yet ultimately disappointing sequel, *Teen Wolf Too?*)

BEACHES?

I have many, but one of them is *PCU*. It stars the deliciously witty Jeremy Piven as "Droz" (before mercury poisoning made him weird) and an almost indistinguishable, pre-Swingers Jon Favreau as "Gutter." (Why indistinguishable? Well, let's just say this was during Jon's "husky" phase. He also has an unfortunate case of dreadlocks.)

PCU is a snapshot into the weekend college visit of incoming freshman Tom Lawrence. Tom is befriended by Droz, and your typical, slapstick, college-themed humor ensues. Think of *PCU* as a poorly done nineties version of *Animal House*, with George Clinton and the P. Funk All-Stars making an appearance. (The nineties *loved* George Clinton.) *Citizen Kane* it ain't, but much like falling in love, you don't get to choose what guilty pleasure movies you end up falling for.

In one of the opening scenes of the movie, we're introduced to Pigman, a student who's writing his senior thesis on the Caine-Hackman theory. The completely fictitious theory claims no matter what time of day it is, you can find Michael Caine or Gene Hackman on TV. To "prove" the theory, Pigman is forced to watch TV twenty-four hours a day, seven days a week.

Pigman is everything you'd expect from someone who constantly watches television with no breaks. Sunken eyes, disheveled hair, filthy clothes, emaciated appearance—he looks dreadful. In the film, he was completely cut off from all human interaction: literally shoved in the corner, set in front of a TV, and forgotten about.

The premise is so preposterous, but Pigman serves as a powerful metaphor for what happens when human beings cannot disconnect. It's been over a decade since I last saw the film, but the imagery surrounding Pigman's character was burned deep into my brain. I'm sure the producers of the film didn't intend for this character to serve as a metaphor, cautioning against the negative psychological, social, and emotional effects of too much media consumption. Nevertheless, the message, for me at least, was loud and clear.

Intuitively, I think most of us understand the warning our mothers gave us that watching too much television isn't good for us. For good reason. Research suggests the human brain is more active during sleep than while watching television.[1] Think about that for a minute. Your brain has more activity while you're unconscious than when you're catching the latest episode of *Here Comes Honey Boo Boo*.

Why is this? The answer is simple: imagination. When the brain watches television (or, more precisely, when your eyes inform your brain that you're watching television), your imagination doesn't have to do any work. Everything is played out visually, nice and neat, right in front of you. The producers, directors, and actors tell your brain what to think. You have no active role. You are, quite literally, a couch potato.

Contrast this with reading a book. When you read, your imagination has to fill in the details. *What does District 13 look like? Just how big is JAWS? How deep does the rabbit hole go?* Your imagination gets to run amok, fantasizing about every last detail. (Sidenote: This is why most people say things like, "The book was way better!" after a novel makes the jump to the big screen.)

SETTING SOCIAL MEDIA LIMITS

In the same way watching television 24/7 would be less than optimal for any individual, the same caution applies to social media. There are times and places to engage with our online communities. Admittedly, the line is very fine for me most of the time.

Some of us are so connected to our devices and online worlds, we're taking it a little too far. We can't live without regular interaction with our social networks. In fact, digital detox retreats are popping up all over the country. With good reason, too: the Internet is rewiring our brains.

Benjamin Kunkel writes in book review:

> The Internet, as its proponents rightly remind us, makes for variety and convenience; it does not force anything upon you. Only it turns out it doesn't feel like that at all. We don't feel as if we had freely chosen our online practices. We feel instead that they are habits we have helplessly picked up or that history has enforced, that we are not distributing our attention as we intend or even like to.[2]

Researchers Michael A. Woodley of Vrije Universiteit in Brussels, Jan te Nijenhuis of the University of Amsterdam, and

Raegan Murphy of the University College Cork in Ireland conducted a meta-analysis of the slowing of simple reaction time, an
indication of general intelligence. They remarked:

> The Victorian Era was marked by an explosion of innova-
> tion and genius, per capita rates of which appear to have
> declined subsequently. The presence of dysgenic fertility
> for IQ amongst Western nations, starting in the 19th
> century, suggests that these trends might be related to
> declining IQ. This is because high-IQ people are more
> productive and more creative. We tested the hypothesis
> that the Victorians were cleverer than modern popula-
> tions, using high-quality instruments, namely measures
> of simple visual reaction time in a meta-analytic study.

While their report certainly doesn't prove causation, there
does seem to be some correlation (the more we outsource to
the social web, the less we have to rely on our gray matter meat
computers). In short, we're getting dumber. Our collective IQ is
dropping by an average of .14 points per year, or 14.1 points in
the last century.[3] This means that the good folks of *Downton Ab-
bey* don't just *sound* smarter than you, they *are* smarter than you.

I had firsthand experience with this scenario in my Greek
class at Bethel Seminary. If you've never taken biblical Greek,
I don't recommend it. It was, without a doubt, the hardest
academic class I've ever taken. Parsing verbs, memorizing word
definitions, proper syntax, learning a whole new alphabet—I literally felt like a dolt. Like I didn't have a brain cell to my name.
There were days I felt like crying (and may have on one occasion,
but it was probably just some dust in my eye).

Sitting in class one afternoon, our professor said to us, "I'm
thinking of changing the textbook for this class."

Praise God! I thought. *Maybe he'll give us something more readable, not so robotic. Something with a little panache, some swagger. Maybe he'll pick a book that doesn't leave me feeling like "If I only had a brain . . ." Maybe I can do this Greek thing after all!*

Then he explained why he was making the change. "I've been reviewing our book with some of my colleagues, and I'm afraid it's too simple."

Um, what? Excuse me? I'm sorry, I thought you just said the book that's been literally causing my hair to fall out of my head is too simple.

"After researching, I found out the material in this book is at the same reading level of the books they used to teach Greek to sixth-graders in the 1920s. Can you believe that?"

I wanted to claw his eyes out with my bare hands. It's one thing to not understand subject material. It's another to be told pre-pubescent children from the past could run mental laps around your slow, slogging, electronically dulled, rapidly shrinking brain.

After the uproar died down (and there was an actual uproar), it started to settle in that I wasn't as smart as I thought I was. Neither were the people around me, many whom I considered to have some of the sharpest minds I'd ever interacted with. A class discussion emerged and we traced our collective lack of mental prowess to one thing: the Internet (a.k.a. an all-encompassing term for anything technology-related). Seriously.

Think about it: how many phone numbers can you rattle off from memory? If you're anything like me, the answer is less than five. Why is this? Because I don't need to remember them anymore. My smartphone does it for me.

In fact, many seminaries are switching from teaching students actual Greek and instead teaching them how to use interpretive Bible software. So instead of learning how to parse the different forms of *doulos*, you'd learn how to use the app that parsed the different forms of *doulos* for you. See the difference? The memory slip begins to make sense now.

Extrapolate this scenario across the entirety of social web, and it's easy to see how human brain-processing power has petered out over the last 100 years. We're overly connected and yet more disconnected than ever. We may "know more" in a quantifiable sense, but at what cost? Can we truly *know* something if we're simply entering a question into a search engine and mindlessly consuming the results given to us? Again, the words of Agent Smith echo in my mind: *This really became [the machines'] world when we started thinking for you.*

Whether you're a person of faith or not, I think we all sense when we go over the line with technology and social media; when we're unable to disconnect. Like canaries in a mine shaft, human beings are remarkably efficient at sensing when we need to put up guardrails. Websites like Do Nothing for Two Minutes[4] implore users to start the site timer, sit back, and do nothing (for two minutes). Popular movements like the National Day of Unplugging[5] ask Internet users to sign a pledge declaring they will disconnect for a full twenty-four hours—no cheating. Further, aforementioned "digital detox" retreats are springing up all over the world—*Huffington Post* mentions a yoga retreat company that offers a 15 percent off to participants willing to give up their iPhones upon arrival, and a Caribbean country with digital detox packages plus a life coach to help you take control over your technology use.[6] We've feasted at the technology table and now, as it were, we've pushed back, unbuttoned.

In church circles, every so often you'll hear of pastors or other public Christian figures declaring they're doing a "social media fast," disconnecting from social networks for a certain length of time. (Never mind that Jesus said, "When you fast, don't make it obvious, as the hypocrites do, for they try to look miserable . . . so people will admire them for their fasting."[7] Publicly declaring a fast is like publicly declaring when you unfollow someone on Twitter. There's a deeper need below the surface, usually based in a need for attention or recognition.)

Regardless of how we're all trying to figure out how to integrate this new technology—this new movement—into our lives. We get it right. We get it wrong. We try again.

It is here where I believe the church has a unique opportunity to lead people to a place of stillness and relearning how to connect with our Maker. If we're willing, we can lead the conversation and model how to have a healthy relationship with the technology we've created.

"IT'S HARD TO WASH FEET OVER SOCIAL MEDIA"

Adorned with spectacles and a white beard of wisdom, Bishop Mark Hanson of the Evangelical Lutheran Church in America believes the most important question a Christian can ask when engaging with social media isn't, "What's healthy?" but "Who is here?" Hanson explains, "The question that I always ask is, 'Who is not at the table?' 'Who's not hearing the Word?' Because absent that person, the kingdom is not complete, the work is not done."

For Bishop Hanson, the dangers of social media (or technology—more broadly speaking) aren't pragmatic (e.g., Do I need to spend less time online?), but sociological. "Twenty years ago sociologists said, 'No longer will we be defined in classes by race, gender, sexual orientation, or economics, it will be by how you get and receive and share information.' I look at [the] older members [in ELCA churches], some of whom are very savvy and stay connected and see all the gifts that come through social media, and others feel marginalized."

Bishop Hanson continued, "We have a new stratification of relationships around social media. [This new system] doesn't have the radical sense of the unity of the body of Christ. It naturally omits diversity."[8] Now, as in times past, the ability to communicate is linked to power. It always has been and, as we can clearly see, always will be.

The lucky few who own the means to communicate a message (*any* message, really) are the ones who will work hardest to protect their investment. Those in power prefer to stay in power. In Luther's day, the tool used to create and maintain power was the printing press. In the early part of the twenty-first century, the tools have changed to a laptop and a solid Internet connection. You may not realize it, but if you own a computer and use it to connect to the web, you're one of the most powerful people on the planet.

For the record, power doesn't need to be a pejorative term. Power—more specifically the ability to control situations to suit one's desired outcome—exists. Like falling in love, friend requests, or awkward family photos, power is an inevitable by-product of human relationships. Those with power choose how they use it.

In this particular context, the ones with power are those who best understand the current methods of communication. Culturally speaking, anything "new" is closely tied with youth culture. In many instances, if there's an emerging trend cutting through culture, you can find young people behind the steering wheel. With social media, this trend certainly proves accurate. In an ironic twist, digital natives (Millennials born between 1980–2001) are at the bottom of the totem pole in many organizational struc-tures, yet possess the ability to communicate a message most ef-fectively and efficiently. Makes one wonder who's truly in charge, doesn't it? In short, social media certainly favors the youth.

However, caring for the "least of these," in the context of technology and social media, is of utmost importance for Han-son. "We have an audience [in the ELCA], who wants to hear about their church in a print form . . . so we're going to live in that world, which is a hard world to live in economically. But what I see happening now, which I'm intrigued by, is the increasingly interactive capacity of the church to facilitate multiple conversa-tions and link multiple conversations out of their self-interest."[9]

In other words, conversations that begin in print blend seamlessly into digital, and vice versa. While older congrega-tion members may prefer a printed weekly bulletin they can scan through and stick in their Bibles, they're learning new ways of communication. They're taking risks like signing up for email newsletters, sending out tweets, and friending their kids on Face-book. This act of humility (and yes, it is humbling for an older adult to have to ask one of their kids to explain "the Facebook") needs to be recognized and commended by younger generations.

The words of Jesus ring especially true in this setting: "In this world the kings and great men lord it over their people, yet they are called 'friends of the people.' *But among you it will be dif-ferent.* Those who are the greatest among you should take the lowest rank, and the leader should be like a servant"[10] (emphasis mine). In the world of Jesus, those who hold the most power *will-ingly* give it up for the sake of those who don't. The information gap is wide open for exploitation at the hands of those in power. Our Lord commands us to take the position of a servant.

In speaking with Bishop Hanson, I believe he rightly critiques the narcissistic nature of social media. "Luther said sin is life curved in on itself. There is a lot of 'curving' in social media. It just reinforces people . . . have a need to be self-absorbed to the point that we're sharing things about our life that, really, does anybody care?" Social media catalyzes the "me first" nature of sin. It accentuates our selfishness and destructive need for ego inflation. For example, you and I both know people whose Instagram feeds are filled with nothing more than self-indulgent selfies and painfully pithy quotes—sometimes they're even quoting themselves! This is one side of the ditch we'd do well to avoid.

But it is also our responsibility to find ways to leverage social technology for our benefit, rather than our detriment. After all, social media isn't going away anytime soon. If we don't redeem it, who will?

Bishop Hanson spoke into the redemptive nature of social media by saying, "[It] gives you all kinds of access to share the good news with someone who isn't going to come near a church to hear it."[11] The shift toward social allows us to rub elbows with all sorts of new and interesting people. Just browsing through my Twitter feed, I'm talking with folks from Minneapolis, Denver, Atlanta, Chicago, New York City, and Canada—CANADA!—all from my little coffee shop perch here in Des Moines. I find that fascinating and world-changing, all at the same time.

When we look at "online community" in regard to the church, it is a complete and total mistake to classify these connections as "not real." As my friend Dave tweeted during the Lenten season, "I don't understand giving up social media for Lent. It's like giving up community/relationship for Lent. Strange choice." The replies to his tweet were telling. Here are a few of them:

- "Yes!!!!!!!!"

- "I see your point, for me it's about the TIME spent on social media that I will spend quietly & introspectively seeking Him."

- "I suppose it depends on what you define as true and authentic community."

Dave smartly punctuated the conversation by saying, "I understand giving up impulsively checking FB & Twitter, but I learn so much about my extended community there . . . It's just part of community for me now."

Herein lies the tension. Dave can and does find community on platforms like Twitter, Facebook, LinkedIn, Pinterest, YouTube, and the myriad of social networks available. You might be reading this book and have an entirely different idea of what does and does not constitute as community. While understandable, we must remember new media cultural values aren't good or bad—they just *are*. Different isn't bad. Different is just different.

Dave is my former college roommate, and Twitter is one of the main relational lines I use to stay connected to him. He lives in Chicago. I live in Des Moines. While many of the relationships I formed at college have faded, Dave and I can still see what's going on with each other, 140 characters at a time. The next time we meet, we'll know, in part, some of the details of what's going on with each other. This is to be affirmed and celebrated. I'm able to go deeper faster with Dave the next time we connect.

We also need to be honest with the reality that online community has limitations. I cannot hug you via Twitter (and I'm a hugger, so that's a problem). I cannot break bread with you in a Facebook group (and by "bread" I mean real, tangible, put-it-in-your-mouth-and-chew bread. Virtual bread loafs don't count!). Further, I can't truly share in your sorrow or suffering in an online environment. I can get close, but there's an obvious threshold. We haven't figured out teleportation (yet).

Sharing in grief or joy at the deepest level requires a physical presence. Always. Offline trumps online.

This makes sense though, doesn't it? God wired us this way: to be present. Think of the life of Jesus. God, being God, could have chosen to redeem the world any way he saw fit.

He could have waved a magic wand.

Or snapped his fingers.

Or simply decreed it to be so from his throne room in heaven, "REDEEMED!"

But he didn't.

He chose to become like you and me—to be *physically present* with the people he came to redeem. There was a gap between God and humanity that could only be closed by his presence. We needed to see his face, hear his heartbeat, touch the hem of his garment, and watch the blood flow from his veins. There is an inherent *carnality* to the gospel message, one that cannot be fully translated online. We are indeed the body of Christ. Again, we can get close, but we can't get all the way. "You can't get there from here!" as the saying goes.

I suppose the inherent danger of online communities is when there is a mistaken belief they can serve as a one-for-one replacement for in-person communities. They can't (and shouldn't). Offline trumps online.

Having said that, online community is definitely preferable to no community whatsoever. Lives have been changed, saved, and redeemed all because gospel-centered online communities exist. It is up to the Christian and his or her local community to discern where and how the lines are drawn. In the words of St. Paul, "'Everything is permissible'—but not everything is beneficial."[12]

I'll close this chapter with some parting words from Bishop Hanson. I believe it sums up the tension between online and offline communities perfectly. "There is something about being with one in silence and the lament. I'm one who believes in communal lament, communal acts of repentance, as well as service and proclamation. Some of the most powerful moments I've had is when I can wash another person's feet as a public act of repentance. It's hard to wash feet through social media."[13]

12

NAVIGATING THE GENERATIONAL DIGITAL DIVIDE

LET'S GET HONEST WITH ourselves for a moment: there's a generational rift in our churches and no one wants to talk about it.

Young leaders have embraced a new way of being the church, fueled by the evolution of social technology. Older leaders, having decades of experience under their belts, are hesitant to "upset the apple cart," so to speak and change the methods that have changed lives and created real change in their churches. I speak with many leaders, both young and old, who find themselves on either side of the generational divide, unwilling to move toward their intergenerational counterparts. (For the record, young leaders can be resistant to the changes social has brought into our churches; conversely, established leaders can be some of the biggest proponents for digital.)

One church I spoke with had a senior leader who banned all electronic devices at staff meetings. On the surface, the benefits from doing this are clear: free from distraction, increased eye contact amongst team members, increased focus on the task at hand. Right? In hearing from the affected staff members, however, the motives for the leader's actions were clear: he didn't use the technology and didn't see the value in it. What this leader failed to realize was many of his staff used their tablet computers and mobile devices for note taking and task management. For those staff members, having these devices banned was akin to having pens and paper banned.

There's also the leader who, after learning about the profound communication style differences between himself and the younger members of his staff, said, "I could move more in their direction, but everything I'm reading says to clamp the vise down harder. Don't budge an inch." Two things: (1) What awful management material is sitting on his coffee table? (2) I wonder how that's working for him? I seem to remember someone very wise once saying those in authority shouldn't flaunt their power over those under them. . . . Something about true leadership being rooted in serving rather than exerting power. . . . Ah, it's probably nothing. I digress.

Finally, there are situations too numerous to count where young leaders become disenfranchised with senior leadership and, instead of faithfully working through differences, disengage and plant their own church. "We feel like God is calling us to start a new church," is usually code for "I'm taking my ball and going home." Certainly there are tons of examples of healthy church plants, but a mentor once said to me, "God typically works by calling us *to* something, not *away* from something." Whenever possible, young leaders who feel the call to plant should do so under the blessing and charge of senior leadership.

There have always been differences amongst the generations. Older folks forget what it's like to be young; younger folks believe they have the answers for everything (and thereby do not need the wisdom of their seasoned brothers and sisters). Preferences over worship guidelines (pipe organ or full band?), attire (come as you are or dressed to the nines?), and preaching style (expository, narrative, or commentary?) have always presented a lively discussion between generations. It boils down to a battle between what is new and untested and what has worked and is proven.

GENERATIONAL TUG-OF-WAR

But one challenge facing church leadership has not been present in generations past—several of them, in fact. As we've seen, we're facing a revolution in the way human beings communicate. Combine this with the retiring baby boomer generation (Americans born between 1946 and 1964), and we've got ourselves a perfect storm: change in communication methods, transition in leadership, and social cultural shifts as far as the eye can see.

If the tension is real (it is), it must be identified in churches, brought out into the open, acknowledged, and discussed. As my dear friend Michelle once told me, "The secret of the universe is in the true naming of things." I suggest there is a way for leaders to gather around the proverbial table and start talking about the changes facing their local churches in a way that's honorable and progressive. "Honorable" to ensure mature leaders feel listened to, heard, and had their experience respected. "Progressive" to give emerging leaders the ability to experiment with new strategies in a significant way.

First, there must be a "willing sense of disbelief." In college, I was part of an improv drama troupe, and this was rule number one: when setting the ground rules with the audience, we asked them to both acknowledge and suspend the categorization mechanism all of us inherently use. This "mechanism" is mostly there to keep us from going insane (literally), but it's also where stereotypes and prejudice emerge from. If one was to enjoy improv, they had to willingly suspend judgment of what they saw on stage. For instance, a male may play the part of a female; a college student may play the role of someone in a nursing home, etc. The challenge was to see past the outside labels and get to the essence of the message being acted out.

Most churches could learn a thing or two from my improv group. Both leadership groups, emerging and mature, come to the table with a set of deeply ingrained presumptions about the other. Older leaders think quietly (and not so quietly, sometimes): *They don't know what they're doing. They're going to ruin everything we've worked so hard to build. I don't understand why they do it that way. Who do they think they are? This is weird. This is strange. What are people going to think? What if everyone forgets about me?*

Younger leaders, for their turn, say to themselves (usually to themselves): *Why don't they just get out of the way? These people are so clueless and out of it! They're just holding me back, resistant to change. If I was in charge, things would be much different . . . real change would happen!*

I probably don't need to tell you this, but neither of these positions is entirely helpful. They're combative, counterproductive, antagonistic, and hurtful. It puts two groups within the same team against each other. A church leadership civil war. You may not be experiencing this dynamic in your church, and if you're not, praise God for the grace in those relationships. But after visiting churches across the country, I can tell you, from experience, this generational tug-of-war is prevalent in many churches; the majority, in fact. (There are also a great many mature leaders who are so disconnected from their staff that they believe there is no problem when there is. A large one, in fact. Aloofness and denial make for powerful insulators.)

To move forward from this struggle, church leaders, both young and old, need to first reconcile they're on the same team. Grab someone who's in a different age group than you, look them in the eye, and say, "My way is different than yours. This does not make it better or worse. We're on the same team!"

In many cases, the tension isn't evident to the degree where there's open conflict. But it's bubbling just below the surface in many contexts. In the same way spouses need to talk through conflict—even seemingly insignificant disagreements—to prevent a blowout further down the road, wise church staff members will engage in this communications exercise before the challenges boil over.

Next you'll need to establish the common purpose or mission both sides believe in. This can be a mission statement, a churchwide goal, anything both sides of the aisle can point to and say, "We're going that way!" This is absolutely essential before moving forward. Many churches have conflict amongst generations not because of communication styles but because there are no common goals to be working toward. Sure, there are vague mission statements hanging on a placard somewhere or mindlessly thrown at the top of church letterhead to give the illusion of unity. But those statements have the sizzle of a cold bowl of oatmeal: lifeless, gloopy, gray mush.

WE ALL WANT THE SAME THING

It is my belief that each local church has a call specific to their community. You and I unite with the purpose of the church universal, yet we have separate and unique callings for our individual lives. Same holds true for many churches. Each one contributes to the larger gospel story God is telling throughout history. Yet each local church has a unique calling specific to the time and place the community it finds itself in.

Again, many churches never do the hard work of drilling down and establishing their purpose. For good reason, too. It's hard work. It's uncomfortable to have the discussions that emerge from asking, "What's our purpose?" Feelings get hurt and ideas get trampled on. Chipping away at calcified assumptions is arduous work.

But the churches who do this go through a transformation process that strengthens connections both to God and to one another. I've seen it happen time and again. They emerge on the other side with a fresh, renewed sense of purpose and possess a unity that only comes by passing through the fires of refinement.

Establishing purpose facilitates a more effective goal formation process. It is here where the rubber meets the road. Goals serve as the fuel for combustion to go from where you are to where you want to be. Once goals are established, units of measurement can be put in place to establish a track record. Results are a language people of any generation can speak, regardless of what side of the digital divide one finds himself or herself on.

Take Vacation Bible School for instance. If a church wants to increase enrollment at VBS, traditionally they may go about it a few different ways. There are the methods you'd expect: increased announcements on the weekends, "invite a friend!" pamphlets disbursed to kids during Sunday school, direct mail marketing campaigns with professionally designed postcards with the dates, times, and locations printed on them. These methods are continually used because they've garnered success.

Then there are the methods an emerging generation would use to get the word out: savvy email-marketing campaigns, complete with landing pages and automated drip-marketing emails, online registration for VBS, complete with online payment integration, and interactive digital VBS invites, optimized specifically for the social web. Increasingly, these are methods that produce desirable results as well. One church we worked with saw a 30 percent increase in VBS registrations after moving from a paper registration and payment system to an online, automated one. They got the word out by using the invite function on Facebook.

Here's the critical point: leaders may have different *methods* for achieving goals, but the *results*, regardless of how they were garnered, speak for themselves. I don't know a single leader who wouldn't welcome a 30 percent increase in VBS attendance. Young, old, or somewhere in between, leaders of any generation can agree the more kids who hear the name "Jesus," the better.

This same dynamic holds true across every spectrum of church life. No matter what the goal is—increased membership, increased tithes and offerings, increased engagement in small groups—leaders speak the common language of results. That way, when younger leaders use a method unfamiliar to mature leadership, they can point back to results (or lack of them, for that matter) and "show their work." Methods like social media marketing, email campaigns, and text message alerts may not make sense to mature leaders, but ministry movement will.

DIGITAL NATIVES AND DIGITAL IMMIGRANTS

It would be easy to write off the differences we've been talking about as an "old vs. young" battle. New school vs. old school. 2Pac vs. Grandmaster Flash. But it's an oversimplification to say young leaders will automatically understand how to apply social networking principles to ministry goals and mature leaders will not. There is parity amongst the generations, to be sure. But native levels of understanding appear whenever a new era of communication emerges. There will be digital natives (typically younger leaders, but not always) and digital immigrants (typically older leaders, again, not always).

A word to emerging leaders. I know a little bit how you feel. You have the passion, energy, and get-up-and-go to make the world you envision a reality. You've got great ideas and the desire to see them come to life. However, those "in charge" may be encouraging you to redirect your best ideas, asking you to rethink or reshape them. For others of you, there's no encouragement to be found from your leaders. Find ways to do what they're asking you to do anyways.

You may feel discouraged, undervalued, unnoticed, or underappreciated. It may feel like you're sitting at the kiddie table during Thanksgiving dinner. All the "grown-ups" discuss the things that matter while you're getting peas flung at you by little cousin Johnny. I know, I've been there. It's frustrating, lonely, and downright maddening at times. Part of the reason you feel frustrated is because no one took the time to invest in you and show you how things work. You don't have to make the same mistake. Don't ever do something without teaching and bringing others along at the same time. Build your legacy from the very start.

It may feel like you're never going to get anywhere. Like you're stuck in mud. Like no one understands what you see or how quickly things are changing. Rest assured. Your time to take the baton is fast approaching; much quicker than you probably think.

In the meantime, find new ways to do the tasks and responsibility entrusted to you. Set up systems and processes that allow you to measure your results. Track endlessly and don't do any-thing strategically that doesn't relate back to a common goal shared by everyone on leadership. If there are no common goals, suggest them. Don't be afraid. You've got more than you realize and more people are on your side than you think.

Above all, know the mature leaders around your team, deep down, are *for you*. They may not know how to verbalize it or dem-onstrate it, but they are *for you*. Even the one who you think hates you—that person is *for you*. How can I be so sure? Because God wired it up that way. We are naturally inclined to build our legacy, and the only way those in leadership above you can do that is *through you*. Sure, funky things like jealousy, fear, envy, strife, confusion, and patronization may get in the way, but ultimately they want you to succeed. Believe it and live out of this reality.

A word to mature leaders. You may be frustrated with the sometimes maddening allegiance your younger colleagues show toward all things digital, but remember, this is all they know. They have grown up in a world very different from yours and, just as you're fearful about adopting this new style of communi-cating, they're just as fearful. Fearful they'll never get a chance to show what they can do before it's too late. They want to work with you, partnering together in ministry to build God's king-dom. They call it "Generation We" for a reason.

Please, make the first move. It will require swallowing your pride and taking the risk to appear foolish. You may not have all the answers; neither do they. Don't feel like you need to be an expert to discuss ministry implications of digital communication with your younger teammates. Sometimes, the most refreshing thing to hear from senior leadership is, "I don't know *why* this works, but I know it's not going away. How can we work together to make it work for us?"

Don't saddle David with Saul's armor. You know the story. In 1 Samuel 18, David is about to fight Goliath—his first real leadership test. Saul says to David, "Listen, I've been in countless battles and fought many men. My armor is the best around—it will keep you safe!" But David tries it on and says, "This doesn't fit," after which he proceeded to pick up five stones and a sling. You know the rest of the story. Slaying Goliath was one of David's most notable achievements. But what would have happened if Saul forced the issue and mandated that David do things his way? He certainly could have, but he didn't. David did things his own way using the tools he knew best and he was wildly successful.

The moral? What worked for Saul didn't work for David. Sometimes your experience as a mature leader, as vast and varied as it might be, actually hinders the effectiveness of your younger colleagues. No amount of life or leadership experience can match when God is doing a new thing on the Earth. Your job, then, is to discern when your wisdom is helpful and, like Saul with David, when it only gets in the way. Doing this is easier said than done, but it's the only way to succeed.

Resource your gunners. There are people on your church staff or in your congregation who understand the digital shift better than you or anyone else in leadership. Find who those people are and ask them, "What do you need to succeed?" Then, when they tell you, give it to them. Risk more than you're comfortable with. If you need to dial it back a few months down the road, you can do so. Nothing takes the wind of an eager young leader's sails more than red tape, bureaucracy, hoops, and hurdles. Allow them to fail fast and often. You are there to provide the guardrails, not to prevent the crash (or worse, not even give them the keys in the first place!).

IT'S ALL ABOUT CONTEXT

I was speaking at an event in San Diego recently, facilitating a discussion with hundreds of church communicators. As I was about to move on to the next point in my slide deck, I saw a lone hand go up in the air out of my peripheral vision. The person hadn't been vocal up to that point, so I wanted to make sure we covered his question before moving on.

"Yes, sir!" I said. He began speaking, but almost immediately I wished I had moved on to the next point. He wasn't loud, obnoxious, or rude. Quite the opposite, in fact. In a quiet, concerned voice, he said, "Justin, this is nice material. But what am I supposed to do when most of the people in my church refuse to embrace anything related to the Internet? They want a paper bulletin every week and nothing else. I don't know what to do." His question was filled with as much fear as it was pain and fatigue. You could tell by the tone of his voice he had been fighting this battle for a long time and was ready to acquiesce. The digital non-natives refused to immigrate to the Promised Land, and this poor leader didn't have anyone to hold his arms up. He was, in a word, defeated.

You could feel the air suck out of the room. I sensed his question placed a finger on a very painful boil most everyone else in the room was experiencing on some level. I could feel hundreds of eyeballs staring at me as if to say, "What does your slide deck have to say about *that*, hmm?" As a presenter, these moments are the most challenging (you have to go off-script) but often lead to the biggest breakthroughs. This experience was no different.

After he first described his situation and asked his question, part earnest and part rhetorical, I must admit in my mind I was thinking, "What an incredibly selfish and self-centered congregation this poor man is serving." A group of people who refuse to change for the sake of unfamiliarity isn't a congregation; it's an angry mob. As with most mobs, rational logic rarely prevails.

As I was still perceiving the weight of his situation, another hand rose high in the air, not too far from where this gentleman was seated. I looked and saw an older woman with salt-and-pepper hair and a soft demeanor and eagerly called on her. Out from beneath a soft Southern drawl burst the words that changed the entire direction of the conversation. She said, "The changes you need to make can only happen in the context of relationship. And that's all there's left to say about that."

It was like Marie Barone from *Everybody Loves Raymond* came in with the drawl and vocabulary of Forrest Gump and punched everyone right in the mouth. The words sank into the crowd the same way living room carpet absorbs spilled red Kool-Aid: slowly at first, then there's not much you can do to get it out. We sat in stunned silence.

I was so shocked because I had never thought of it that way before. This poor pastor was pleading with his congregation to make changes they didn't want to make. Only, they had no frame of reference for *why* they needed to make the changes. They just knew if they changed, things would get more difficult.

Take that same pastor and give him the same request and, instead of pleading and begging for online communication adoption, imagine he put it in a relational context. Imagine he said something like this on a Sunday morning:

"Everyone, I want to talk to you about something I've been thinking about lately. There is an entire generation of young people out there who don't know the comfort, peace, joy, and happiness that our church community provides its members. They don't know you and your amazing families. They don't know your stories. They don't know the joy of being in relationship with you.

"I know many of you have kids and grandkids whom you love dearly. I want you to picture one of them—doesn't matter who—just picture one of your children or a grandchildren. Now, imagine you needed to get an urgent message to them. This message is of critical importance. It might even make a difference between life and death.

"Because you're good parents and grandparents, I know you'd move heaven and earth to find a way to communicate to them. It wouldn't matter if the phones were out, if FedEx was on strike, or if the Internet disappeared overnight—you'd find a way to reach them, wouldn't you? You'd figure out how to best connect them to your message.

"The way we're communicating our message as a church, the way we're telling our story, has suited us well for decades. But I'm starting to sense shift and I need your help to move forward. I want you to look around for a moment. You may have noticed we're all getting a little older and our community, well, it isn't getting any younger. That's because young people have new ways of telling their stories, many of which are very different than the ones we're comfortable with.

"Will you join me? Will you help me tell the story of our church in new ways? Remember, a younger generation—the generation of your children and grandchildren—is depending on us to reach them. What will your answer to them be?"

13

CHIPPING AWAY THE LAYERS

LISTEN TO WHAT *Wall Street Journal* blogger Gary Hamel says about the church,

> Over the centuries, religion has become institutionalized, and in the process encrusted with elaborate hierarchies, top-heavy bureaucracies, highly specialized roles and reflexive routines. Religion won't regain its relevance until church leaders chip off these calcified layers, rediscover their sense of mission, and set themselves free to reinvent "church" for a new age. Doing this is going to take a management revolution. Back in the first century, the Christian church was organic, communal and mostly free of ritual—and it needs to become so again.[1]

Hamel also said in his lecture at Leadership Summit in 2009, "The web is post-bureaucratic structure," and, "Churches need to be fervent and flexible communities—participatory and open source [much like the web]." I find this terribly refreshing. So do many in the new media culture. Sharing is baked into the very nature of who they are, so discerning ways to smartly bring two-way dialogue into church services is imperative for leaders to consider as they move forward.

I believe Hamel, much like Martin Luther and Seth Godin, is a heretic. He's willing to push beyond culturally acceptable limits for the sake of causing change. Change often isn't comfortable, but is almost always needed.

Besides, isn't it just like God to have a business management expert break up the crusted-over layers of church leadership and structure? One thing I've learned while working with churches across the country is, while they may take their mission very seriously, they don't take their organizational structure seriously. *At all.* This typically manifests itself in one of two ways: under-structure and over-structure.

In the case of under-structuring, there is little to no thought put into how the church itself will be organized. "If we just preach the gospel, God will take care of the rest!" (or something like that). Practical realities like mortgages, measuring tithes and offerings, and, yes, marketing the church, are ignored under the false pretense of being faithful. It's almost as if God is somehow beholden to bless their ignorance.

Do you know churches like this? I do and it's unbelievably frustrating. I'm sure you've heard the analogy of the man sitting, stranded, on top of his roof as floodwaters rise around his house. He pleads to God for help: *God, please save me! Send help!*

All of a sudden, someone in a rescue boat motors over to the man and says, "Get in!" The man on the roof, however, says, "No! I'm waiting for God to save me!"

Next, a helicopter hovers overhead. They send a rope down to the man as the waters quickly rise around his house. "Grab the rope!" the rescuers shout. The man on the roof, however, says, "NO! I'm waiting for God to save me!"

The floodwaters are too much for the man. They eventually overtake his whole house and sweep him away. He drowns.

When he gets to heaven, the first thing he asks God is, "God! I asked you for help! I really needed you and you didn't come through. *Where were you?*" God's reply: "Son, I was there the whole time. I was the one who sent the man in the rescue boat, the team in the helicopter . . ."

The idea is a little cliché, but you get the point.

In many mainline denominations, a top-down structure is in place. While structure can be helpful and should be encouraged in most church contexts, there is little doubt that hierarchy becomes unhelpful when it solidifies in place and prevents change in the facing of a morphing culture. When churches cannot make critical decisions quickly because of red tape, over-structure is usually the culprit. When our systems of leadership and communication prevent us from responding appropriately to the situation in front of us, the world loses. A new media culture values real-time decision making, and the church has struggled to adapt in this way.

DOING THE WORK OF THE CHURCH OUTSIDE ITS FOUR WALLS

One person who hasn't struggled to adapt is Shaun King. When I sat down with Shaun in a high-rise condo overlooking the New York City skyline, I was reminded of what an unfettered, faith-filled man can do. Shaun is the CEO & Founder of Hope-Mob (@HOPE on Twitter), a social media movement designed to bring generous strangers together from all over the world to rally together around one human story at a time.

Shaun has built an online community with a reach of over half a million fans, followers, and friends. Through HopeMob (a play on the social media-driven term "flash mob") and his personal account, Shaun's social media reach and influence on any given day is vastly larger than most churches' in this country— even the world! When Shaun wants to create change—good, positive, life-affirming change—he simply rolls up his sleeves and asks his social media community to get to work.

Our conversation revolved around a theme of wanting to do good but not wanting to get mired down in regulation. Checks and balances are one thing, but obstinate allegiance to a slogging, slow system is another. Shaun is a man who thinks differently about what it means to be a follower of Jesus, and he's using social media to fuel his message.

As a former senior pastor for Courageous Church in Atlanta, Georgia, Shaun knows what it means to be in ministry. He's preached the sermons, set up seats on Sunday morning, attended budget meetings, and prayed faithfully with the members of his community. In fact, most of his adult life has been spent serving in and around churches.

But in late 2011, Shaun and his wife, Rai, made the painful decision to leave ministry all together. Shaun felt that God was taking his family in a direction that was significantly different than what his church desired. He didn't know it at the time, but the something "significantly different" was HopeMob.

It's difficult to put into words what HopeMob is and does, but I like to think of it as a kick-starter for charity. Shaun describes the foundational idea behind HopeMob: "Our initial goal was just to tell one story at a time of a person or a group of people in need and then allow people to help that one person. Our goal was really just to tell stories of people who aren't being helped anywhere else . . . and we've been able to do that."

A typical project works like this: a story of someone in need is placed on the HopeMob website (*www.hopemob.org*). Projects can range anywhere from a family needing money to pay for their deaf child's hearing aids, to helping buy slaves off the black market, to continued support-raising efforts for the victims of the

2013 Boston Marathon bombings. The amount needed for the project is listed on the story profile, along with how many people have contributed and how much time is left to help fund the goal.

As I listened to Shaun reflect on the tension of leaving the church but still wanting to build God's kingdom, I was struck by this statement:

> I felt like my role as a pastor—the role of any pastor or religious leader, in a lot of ways—is to teach people how to pray, how to live. With HopeMob, our goal is to be an answer to people's prayers.[2]

Shaun will be the first one to tell you HopeMob isn't a faith-based charity. No sermons are preached, no crosses affixed to the wall at HopeMob headquarters, no corporate prayer meetings as a staff. But that doesn't mean he checks his faith at the door. With HopeMob, Shaun told me clearly, "I see my job as being an answer to people's prayers."

It should be noted HopeMob runs almost entirely through social media. It's how the movement was built, it's how projects get funded and publicized, it's how Shaun has managed to attract high-profile coverage from places like CNN[3], TechCrunch[4], Mashable[5]—even Oprah has taken notice[6]. Even though Shaun now works with a large team, oftentimes he's personally driving the funding efforts behind many of the projects on the HopeMob website. Shaun says, "I think my calling is empowering other people to see how they can help be the solution to unsolvable problems. That's what gets me going."

He's clearly doing something right. He and his team have built a sprawling online community, with connections literally reaching around the globe. It is this community, many of whom Shaun and the HopeMob team will never meet, that's changing people's lives and, thereby, the world. When you have access to nearly half a million people through social networks like Twitter and Facebook, good works are inevitable with just the right amount of focus.

Like Luther, Shaun isn't shy about asking the "what ifs?" when it comes to cutting-edge technology. He's figured out a way to do kingdom-building work by harnessing the power of social media. He is no Lone Ranger. This isn't a one-man show. It is, however, a look at what happens when a kingdom-minded individual asks God, "How can I serve?" with an openness to new methods.

In closing this chapter, read these words from Shaun and see if it doesn't resemble the ideas Jesus had for his people; for his church. A place where the marginalized gain community, where wounds are healed, where lives are restored, where those on the road to death receive life overflowing, where the kingdom of God advances forcefully, one tweet at a time:

> A lot of the people we help have started to lose faith in humanity in some ways and they've lost hope. What we do, beyond sending resources to them, is we try to give them hope . . . there are good people in the world. There are people who care about you and people that want to make a difference. That makes a big difference. Then what ends up happening is the people we help [through HopeMob] often become huge cheerleaders for the other people on our platform. So we're excited.[7]

14

88 MPH

DO YOU REMEMBER WHERE you were the first time you saw *Back to the Future II*? I was in Cleveland with all my cousins, our annual trip back East to visit relatives in Ohio. (This particular trip was memorable on its own merits. It was the year a beloved family dog, Chaps, nearly tore off my Uncle Doug's hand in a fit of jealous rage after Uncle Doug chose to baste the turkey instead of take Chaps for a walk. Yikes!)

If you haven't seen the movie, (1) Shame on you, (2) It's your typical guy-meets-girl-meets-crazy-loner-vaguely-creepy-mad-scientist-who-builds-a-time-machine-out-of-a-Delorean flick, (3) No, really. Shame on you. One of the clearest memories I have of the movie is thinking about what life would be like all the way in 2015, where the future action takes place. Of note in 2015:

The Cubs win the World Series.

Nike makes shoes with automatic laces.

Clothes automatically tailor themselves to fit the wearer.

And some even say the movie prophesied Google Glass.

Add to the mix the floating skateboards (a.k.a. hoverboards), ovens that make pizza on demand ("hydrate level four, please"), and the video conferencing system in Marty's futuristic home ("Read my fax, 'You're fired!'" featuring the incomparable Flea a.k.a. "Needles"), and you have the stuff my boyhood dreams are made of. It was all a bit too much for a somewhat geeky nine-year-old with an overactive imagination to take in.

I look back on it now and realize the movie wasn't much more than a lighthearted Hollywood attempt to capitalize on a budding successful franchise (the original movie was shot as a stand-alone project). But this experience churned a deep-seated creative imagination within me to visualize the "what if?" The possibilities for the future seemed limitless—everything and anything was possible.

Flying cars. Robot dog-walkers. Video games you play with your mind. Hoverpods to help you get around the house. Where do I sign up?

Don't ask me why this movie was so pivotal. I can't pinpoint the answer other than to say the question "what if?" is a very powerful motivator. Countries have been conquered, endless art has been created, and countless first kisses have happened, all in the name of "what if?" For me, in 1989, in Cleveland, *Back to the Future Part II* gave me eyes to see and helped me imagine the world of "what if?" (The cross-branding promotion with Pizza Hut's "Solar Shades" didn't hurt either.)

WHAT'S YOUR "WHAT IF?"

When we look at the life of the church, I believe we are facing the question of "what if?" right here, right now. In many ways, it's unavoidable. There's a formidable fork forming in the road, forcing the church to choose one way or the other:

"What if we try something new?"

"What if we keep doing things the way they've always been done?"

To be sure, abstaining from a choice isn't an option. Culture moves more like a roaring river than a stagnant side pool. The church can no more remain inactively perched at the fork in the road than a whitewater raft can remain motionless on the rapids of the Colorado River.

What if we learned to use social media in the same way we use the telephone? Or a copier? Or pen and a paper? I'm not being flippant, either. Social media will continue to embed itself into the cultural fabric to the point where organizations that choose *not* to participate will be seen in the same light as the Amish.

What if the church rises up and takes her rightful place in culture as an early adopter of technology? What if we follow the path history has laid out for us, choosing to leverage social technology for the sake of building God's kingdom, rather than shirking from the spotlight afraid of looking foolish?

What if the church blazes the trail for all industries, showing what happens when a powerful message is purposefully translated online to reach as far and as wide as humanly possible?

What if, like St. Paul, Luther, McPherson, Graham, Cynthia Ware, Bishop Michael Hanson, and Shaun King, we seize the technological opportunities in front of us and make an impact far greater than we could ever imagine?

What if we truly believed the charge we received in the garden of Eden? To be co-creators with God, partnering with him to change and shape reality with the tools he brings us.

What if churches began to drill down into their Big Idea? Taking the time needed to solidify a singular purpose for our activity within the kingdom of God? What if we did the hard work of translating our Big Idea online, so a waiting, watching, weary world could hear it?

What if we blazed new trails online instead of following the hard-packed paths?

What if we chose to be simple, absurd, and lived in a way that caused people to ask questions?

What if people who don't know Jesus could come to know him because his church knew how to speak the language of the culture they're called to serve?

"What if?" is a powerful motivator indeed.

Regardless of how the North American Church responds, our fate as the body of Christ is secure: *Victor*. As the church universal, we will not fail. We *cannot* fail. This is most certainly true.

The questions we must answer together are: What role do we want to play in the victory? Do we want to remain idle, sitting on the sidelines watching others play the game? Or do we want to strap on our shoes, get our hands a little dirty, take our lumps, but come out on the other side with the satisfaction of a job well done?

I can think of no better way to close our journey together than with the words of the person who helped spark this desire in me to see the church become social. Once again, Cynthia Ware:

> Although an entirely virtual world might still sound overly futuristic, within a generation or two the world will move from a primarily analog-augmented existence to a digitally dependent one. The effects of the 20th century's Industrial Revolution and its streamlined mass production pale when compared to the potential outworking of the Technological Revolution already under way. Our generation could see transformations we can only imagine—manipulating matter at the atomic level, transcending spatial boundaries, and potentially engineering life. We will be forced to wrestle these impending

ethical challenges, seeking the heart of God for situations with no historical precedents. . . . Although high-tech progress appears to be unstoppably self-driven it is, in fact, an expression of human effort. As such, it is therefore subject to the divine orchestration of events leading history towards the fulfillment of all Scripture. The future of the 21st-Century Church, at least, is completely secure.[1]

Roads? Where we're going we don't need roads.
Let's do this.

NOTES

CHAPTER 1 — HERETICS NEEDED: APPLY WITHIN

1. If you go to my speaking page, you'll see a picture of this fabled event taken by the amazing Anthony Barlich. I use it to remind me where things started and that which is my central message.

2. Ephesians 2:8–9 NIV

3. Hebrews 4:16a

4. St. John quoted in Elizabeth L. Eisenstein, *The Printing Press as an Agent of Change*, Volume 1 (Cambridge: Cambridge University Press, 1980), 3.

5. Elizabeth L. Eisenstein, *The Printing Press as an Agent of Change*, Volume 1 (Cambridge: Cambridge University Press, 1980), 317.

6. Seth Godin, *Tribes: We Need You to Lead Us* (New York: Penguin, 2008), 49

7. Jon Acuff, "We Did It! We Raised $60,000 to Build 2 Kindergartens in Vietnam," *Jon Acuff*, December 4, 2009. *www.jonacuff.com/stuffchristianslike/2009/12/we-did-it-we-raised-60000-to-build-2-kindergartens-in-vietnam.*

CHAPTER 2 — CALCULATED RULE-BREAKING

1. Acts 10:44

2. Bob Gale, *Back to the Future Part II*, directed by Robert Zemeckis (Universal City, CA: Universal Studios, 1989).

3. *cainesarcade.com.*

CHAPTER 3 — CAVE WALLS, MARTIANS, AND THE HISTORY OF COMMUNICATION

1. This is debated in some circles, but the strongest scholarly evidence has Matthew as the earliest gospel account.

2. H. G. Wells, adapted by Howard Koch and Anne Froelick, "The War of the Worlds," directed by Orson Welles (New York: Columbia Broadcasting, 1938).

3. David Bourgeois, *Ministry in the Digital Age* (Downers Grove, IL: InterVarsity Press, 2013), 17.

4. Joan of Arc in Steven Kanehl, *I Was Born for This* (Mustang: OK, Tate Publishing, 2008), 89.

5. TV-Free America, "Television & Health," *California State University-Northridge*, 2007. www.csun.edu/science/health/docs/tv&health.html.

6. Normon Herr, "The Industrial Revolution," *California State University-Northridge*, 2007. www4.ncsu.edu/unity/users/p/pwhmds/indrev.html.

7. Tim Chen, "American Household Credit Card Debt Statistics: 2013," March 2013. www.nerdwallet.com/blog/credit-card-data/average-credit-card-debt-household.

8. At face value, these terms could seem to contradict each other. But as Christians living in God's grace, we have all felt the "Here, but not yet" of possessing both Christ's righteousness through faith, and the baggage of the sin that besets us.

9. BBC, "Languages of the World," *BBC Languages*, 2013. www.bbc.co.uk/languages/guide/languages.shtml.

10. Genesis 11:6

11. John Dyer, *From the Garden to the City* (Grand Rapids: Kregel Publications, 2011), 104.

12. Seth Godin, "The Realization Is Now," Typepad, April 23, 2011. sethgodin.typepad.com/seths_blog/2011/04/the-realization-is-here.html.

13. ELCA Office of the Secretary, "ELCA Membership by Year," *ELCA News Service*, 2011. www.elca.org/Who-We-Are/Our-Three-Expressions/Churchwide-Organization/Communication-Services/News/Resources/Stats.aspx.

14. Joe Weisenthal, "The Bear Market in GOD," *Business Insider*, July 2, 2012. www.businessinsider.com/construction-spending-on-religious-institutions-2012-7.

15. Ed Stetzer, "SBC 2011 Statistical Realities–Facts Are Our Friends But These Are Not Very Friendly Facts," *The Exchange*, June 13, 2012. www.christianitytoday.com/edstetzer/2012/june/sbc-2011-statistical-realities--facts-are-our-friends-but.html.

16. NewMedia TrendWatch, "Demographics," Feb–March 2013. www.newmediatrendwatch.com/markets-by-country/17-usa/123-demographics?start=1.

17. Tom Webster, "The Infinite Dial 2012: Navigating Digital Platforms," Edison Research, April 10, 2012. www.edisonresearch.com/home/archives/2012/04/the-infinite-dial-2012-navigating-digital-platforms.php.

18. Emily Brandon, "Retirees Fastest-Growing Users of Social Networks," *US News*, August 30, 2011. money.usnews.com/money/blogs/planning-to-retire/2011/08/30/retirees-fastest-growing-users-of-social-networks.

19. Joshua 24:15

CHAPTER 4 — SIGNS OF THE TIMES

1. Matt Singley, et al., "Church TechCamp Los Angeles," Facebook event, 2008. www.facebook.com/events/24194639939.

2. Opinions vary on generation classification spans, especially since generation identification is fluid. The starting point for Gen Y is 1980 because of the political, social,

and economic climate these individuals were born into. Similarly, 2001 marks the end of Gen Y because of one simple event: 9/11. It marked a significant shift across the globe, spanning nearly every sector of society. Quite simply, individuals born after this date live in a completely different world.

3. Helmut Richard Niebuhr, *The Meaning of Revelation* (Louisville: Westminster John Knox Press, 2006), 25.

4. These concepts of the new media values (interactivity, personalization ubiquity, connectedness, and sharing) that I discuss in chapters 5–8 belong to Cynthia Ware. She has graciously allowed me to share them with you and elaborate on them.

CHAPTER 5 – VALUE 1: LOOKING FOR A MOUSE

1. Clay Shirky, "Web 2.0 Expo SF 2008," *blip*. blip.tv/web2expo/web-2-0-expo-sf-2008-clay-shirky-862384.

2. Kristie Bouryal, "Nielsen and Twitter Establish Social TV Rating," *Nielsen*, December 17, 2012. www.nielsen.com/us/en/insights/press-room/2012/nielsen-and-twitter-establish-social-tv-rating.html

3. Michael Arrington, "Obama Sets Record with January Donations; Online Donations 88% of Total," *Tech Crunch*, February 4, 2008. techcrunch.com/2008/02/04/obama-sets-record-with-january-donations-online-donations-88-of-total.

4. *www.mickmel.com/blog/201011/more-churches-are-on-twitter-but-are-they-listening.*

5. David Roach, "Research: Churches Increasing Efforts in Social Media, Facebook," *LifeWay*, January 21, 2011. www.lifeway.com/Article/LifeWay-Research-Churches-Increasingly-Fans-Facebook-Social-Media.

6. Hebrews 4:12

7. Mem Fox, *Whoever You Are* (Boston: HMH Books for Young Readers, 2006).

8. Donald Miller, "Why I'm Not More Public About My Faith," *Storyline*, February 5, 2013. storylineblog.com/2013/02/05/why-im-not-more-public-about-my-faith.

9. Matthew 6:1 The Message

10. Neil Postman, *Amusing Ourselves to Death* (New York: Penguin, 2005), 7.

11. Greek, "I am, the one speaking to you," referring to the woman's statement in the previous verse.

12. Gary Vaynerchuck, interview by Justin Wise, May 15, 2013.

13. The quote, commonly credited to Martin Luther, has been widely circulated.

CHAPTER 7 – NEW VALUE 3: THE FADING LINE BETWEEN ONLINE AND OFFLINE

1. Tina Fey, *Bossypants* (New York: Little, Brown, 2013), 161.

2. Sarah Hofstetter in Rachel Sanders, "How Oreo Got That Twitter Ad Up So Fast," *BuzzFeed*, February 3, 2013. www.buzzfeed.com/rachelysanders/how-oreo-got-that-twitter-ad-up-so-fast.

3. Cynthia Ware, "Technology and the Virtual Church," *Echo Hub*, June 10, 2008. echo-hub.com/posts/web/technology-and-the-virtual-church.

4. www.nydailynews.com/news/world/check-contrasting-pics-st-peter-square-article-1.1288700.

CHAPTER 8 — VALUE 4: LIFE AMPLIFICATION

1. Thomas L. Friedman, *The World Is Flat* (New York: Macmillan, 2007), 178–79.

2. Mark Hanson, interview by Justin Wise, February 21, 2013.

CHAPTER 9 — THE MEDIUM IS THE MESSAGE (AND THE MESSAGE DOESN'T CHANGE)

1. John Dyer, *From the Garden to the City*, 38.

2. Ibid., 38.

3. Andy Wachowski and Lana Wachowski, *The Matrix* (Burbank, CA: Warner Bros., 1999).

4. Marshall McLuhan, *Understanding Media* (New York: Routledge, 2005), 7.

5. For a great dissection of the impact the mediums we choose have on us, please read John Dyer's amazing book *From the Garden to the City*.

6. Matthew 18:20

7. Matthew 4:19

8. Matthew 5:43–44

9. Matthew 7:1

10. Matthew 7:12

11. John 8:7

12. Martin Luther, *The Life of Luther*, collected by M. Michelet (London: George Bell and Sons, 1898), 293.

13. Neil Postman, *Amusing Ourselves to Death*, 16.

14. Alex Knapp, "Voyager 1 Has Almost Left the Solar System," Forbes, June 30, 2013. www.forbes.com/sites/alexknapp/2013/06/30/voyager-1-has-almost-left-the-solar-system.

15. Genesis 1:27

16. Neil Postman, *Amusing Ourselves to Death*, 9.

17. Ephesians 3:15 NASB

18. Romans 8:29

19. Colossians 1:19

20. Matthew 26:36–46

21. Mark 14:36

22. Luke 22:44

23. Luke 22:42

CHAPTER 10 — PYRAMIDS AREN'T JUST IN EGYPT

1. Psalm 133:2

2. John 5:19

3. Luke 12:49

4. John 11:53

5. Andy Wachowski and Lana Wachowski, *The Matrix*.

6. For a more philosophical discussion regarding social media, please reference the chapter titled "The Medium is the Message (and the Message Doesn't Change)."

7. This was an internal study conducted at Monk Development in which the results were not made public.

8. 1 Thessalonians 5:3

9. Megan O'Neill, "How Netflix Bankrupted and Destroyed Blockbuster," *Business Insider*, March 1, 2011. www.businessinsider.com/how-netflix-bankrupted-and-destroyed-blockbuster-infographic-2011-3.

10. Ed Stetzer, *Planting New Churches in a Postmodern Age* (Nashville: Broadman & Holman, 2003), 10.

11. Dave Hnida, "The Latest on Kevin Ware's Injury," *CBS Denver*, March 31, 2013. http://denver.cbslocal.com/2013/03/31/the-latest-on-kevin-wares-injury/.

CHAPTER 11 — WASHING FEET

1. EUFIC—European Food Information Council, "Watching less TV, being more active and sleeping more is linked to a healthy body weight in young children," *ScienceDaily*, November 16, 2011. www.sciencedaily.com/releases/2011/11/111115175349.htm.

2. Benjamin Kunkel, "Lingering," *n+1*, May 31, 2009. http://nplusonemag.com/lingering.

3. Michael A. Woodley, Jan te Nijenhuis, Reagan Murphy, "Were the Victorians cleverer than us? The decline in general intelligence estimated from a meta-analysis of the slowing of simple reaction time," *Elsevier*, February 27, 3013. http://lezgetreal.com/wp-content/uploads/2013/05/were-the-victorians-smarter-than-us.pdf.

4. www.donothingfor2minutes.com

5. www.nationaldayofunplugging.com

6. Carolyn Gregoire, "Digital Detox Retreat: Unplug & Recharge At 8 Tech-Free Getaways," *Huffington Post*, April 24, 2013. www.huffingtonpost.com/2013/04/24/digital-detox-retreats-un_n_3147448.html.

7. Matthew 6:16

8. Mark Hanson interview.

9. Ibid.

10. Luke 22:25b–26

11. Mark Hanson interview.

12. 1 Corinthians 10:23

13. Mark Hanson interview.

CHAPTER 13 — CHIPPING AWAY THE LAYERS

1. Gary Hamel, "Organized Religion's 'Management Problem,'" *Wall Street Journal Blogs*, August 21, 2009. http://blogs.wsj.com/management/2009/08/21/organized-religions-management-problem/.

2. Shaun King, interview by Justin Wise, March 13, 2013.

3. *http://startingpoint.blogs.cnn.com/2012/04/19/a-flashmob-for-charity-hopemob-org-founder-on-a-new-way-to-give-back/*.

4. *http://techcrunch.com/2012/07/26/finding-inspiration-in-the-aurora-tragedy-by-helping-victims-through-hopemob/*.

5. *http://mashable.com/2012/01/05/hopemob-charity-website/*.

6. *www.oprah.com/blogs/Choreographed-Hope-Brought-to-you-by-HopeMob*.

7. Shaun King interview.

CHAPTER 14 — 88 MPH

1. Cynthia Ware, "Technology and the Virtual Church."

ACKNOWLEDGMENTS

FIRST AND FOREMOST, I want to thank my family.

Certainly my strong and sassy wife, Kerry, my precious son, Finnegan, and my dearest daughter, Evie. This book wouldn't have happened without the many weekend afternoons my wife held down the fort while I went to write. She also read most of this book before anyone else. There's something indescribable about hearing your wife say, "you're a great writer" and mean it. I love you, Buggy!

I also want to thank my mom and dad, Keith and Shirley Wise; my sister and brother-in-law, Kristin (aka Iowa Girl Eats–she's a big deal, look her up!) and Ben Porter; and my dear brother, Ryan (aka Peep). A guy couldn't ask for a better support system. Thank you. I love you!

Ben Arment, you gave me permission to be the person I always wanted to be. I won't forget that.

To Cynthia Ware, thank you for giving me a chance. Thank you for believing in me, correcting me, and molding my early thoughts on what it means to be a digital disciple.

I want to thank my dearest friend and mentor, Megs (aka Michael Meggison). Your encouragement, love, support, and friendship over the past decade (10 YEARS!) has shaped me into the man I am today. Here's to the next 10 years, my friend!

To Mr. Jeffrey Hanson (aka "the most mysterious man in the world"), thank you for teaching me how to go one-on-one with the One.

To Pastor Mike Housholder, I will never forget the day we talked social media and ministry over burgers and fries. Thank you for believing in me, even when others didn't.

To Pastor Richard Webb, thank you for putting up with me and loving me well along the way. I'll just leave it at that =)

Thanks to my friends and family at Lutheran Church of Hope, where most of the early ideas for this book were formed. You loved and nurtured me when I didn't deserve it.

To my Bethel Seminary crew—Adam Bradshaw, Jolly Ray, N8, Brodie Taphorn, Jason DeVries, Chad-O, Brent (or is it Brad?) Osborne, Nic Smith, and Michael Bochman—iPod and Jenius 4 Lyfe. Stumbo, you get your own line because we slept mere feet from each other for years and, hey, that's gotta count for something.

Thank you to Dr. Jeanmine Brown for not only being a great professor, but a great human being as well; thanks to Dr. Kyle Roberts for showing me science and faith are not mutually exclusive; thanks to Dr. Peter Vogt for teaching me "OT" does not mean "Optional Testament"; thanks to Dan Jass for having the guts to say what everyone else was thinking; thanks to Kristen Anderson for being one of the most courageous, kindhearted leaders I've ever met; thanks to Danielle Dworak for making it easy to do something different and Joseph Dworak for making me feel like an all-star.

Thanks to my friends at Monk Development. Drew, for teaching me how to help churches think big; James for always shooting straight; Etienne for laughing at my feeble attempts at a South African accent. To Heidi, Jodi, Beau, Benson, Jenn, Korrie, Chris,

Ricky, Scott, Jennie, TJ, Jennie, Marcie, Autumn, Jesse, Shane, Stayton, JBo, and Adam, thanks for being my friend.

Thanks to Rhett Smith and Jeff Goins for basically forcing Randall to get this book off the ground.

To my beloved Des Moines, no matter where I go, I will always run back into the safety of your arms. You are home.

I want to thank Mars Cafe and Smokey Row for providing the tasty coffee and quiet space to write, think, and create.

Thanks to the Starbucks in St. Catherine's, Ontario, for letting me stay until 3 a.m. to finish the manuscript of this book the day before it was due.

Thanks to Diplo, Krewella, 3LAU, KapSlap, BroSafari, and Kaskade for the tunes. Dance on, my friends.

To the good folks at the Moody Collective—Randall Payleitner, Natalie and Matt Mills, Bailey Utecht, and Pam Pugh—thank you for putting up with me. I hope this book makes you proud. You all deserve it.

Lastly, to you, the reader, I say "thank you." If you've made it this far, we've traveled a lot of ground together. Thanks for joining me in the journey. You've changed my life. Before you go, head to http://justinwise.net/thanks for a small token of my appreciation.

To God be the glory, forever and ever, Amen!

moody
collective

Moody Collective brings words of life to a generation seeking deeper faith. We are a part of Moody Publishers, representing this next generation of followers of Christ through books, blogs, essays, and more.

We seek to know, love, and serve the millennial generation with grace and humility. Each of our books is intended to challenge and encourage our readers as they pursue God. To learn more, visit our website, www.moodycollective.com.

What Did They Say Now? is a weekly conversation between friends. Brian, Courtney, and Barnabas explore ideas and topics, both serious and lighthearted, from a Christian-faith perspective but without all the jargon that so often accompanies it. They are candid, open, and blunt. This podcast plants the seeds of a conversation—join us.

www.whatdidtheysaynow.org